The Red, White & Rosé
of
WINES

BY WILLIAM E. MASSEE

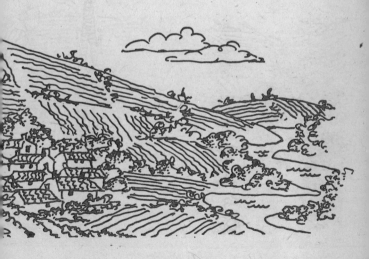

A Dell Book

Published by the
Special Marketing Division
Dell Publishing Co., Inc.
750 Third Avenue, New York, N.Y. 10017
Copyright © 1972 by Dell Publishing Co., Inc.
All rights reserved.
Printed in the United States of America

Drawings: Dorothy Ivens
Design: Angelo Grasso; Ara Derderian

TO THE MEN
WHO MAKE
OUR WINES

CONTENTS

The Red, White & Rosé
of
WINES

HOW TO TELL A GOOD WINE

"I like wine but I'm never sure of which one to get," said the lady. "Tell me what to look for."

All the great wines come from famous European regions, was my answer, so try the table wines imported from France or Italy or Germany, and don't forget Spain and Portugal.

"Already that's too many," said the lady. "You'll have to be more specific."

Start with France, I suggested. Red, white or rosé, French wines are the greatest. Burgundy and Bordeaux are the most famous wine regions, but try the imports from Alsace, the Loire, the Rhone. Any shop will have these low-priced regional wines and others from districts or townships within the regions, and even some from specific vineyards.

Start with Italy. Everybody knows Chianti, but there's Bardolino and Valpolicella, Barolo and Barbera, Valtellina and Lambrusco, among the reds. Among the whites, there's Soave, Orvieto, Frascati. Each district produces distinctive wines.

Start with Germany. All of its best wines are white,

from districts along the Rhine or the Moselle.

Or try imports from Portugal or Spain. Try Portuguese brand names like Mateus, Casal Garcia or Grão Vasco. Just pick out a country or a region or a brand and serve the wine with meals.

"How can I be sure it's going to be good?" asked the lady.

Buy wines from importers you can trust and from shops that have a wide selection and a reputation to protect. Importers are constantly roving the wine regions to find good growers and shippers, tasting every wine before they buy, selecting only the best. For every imported wine on the market there are dozens that don't make the grade. Buyers for major importers may taste a hundred wines to find one they like. The first selective tasting is done for you by experts.

Imported wines are the fashion these days—just because selection is so careful. Some of the vineyards have been famous for a thousand years and more; many of today's growers are descendants of a dozen generations of winemakers. The tradition of good wines is as old as civilization.

"That still doesn't tell me how to tell a good wine," said the lady. "How can I be sure?"

Tasting tells, I answered. A good wine tastes good. It's as simple as that. There will be nothing unpleasant in the taste. But only you can tell. Your best bet is an imported wine from a reputable importer. Wine shops are staffed by knowing people who can help you with selections. You'll find dozens you like.

"I guess I'll have to take your word for that," said the lady.

You can trust your own taste, said I. The more wines you try, the more wines you'll find you like.

Most of us come upon wines by chance, finding some we like and buying them again if we happen to remember the name, finding others that seem too sweet or too dry, perhaps being confused by the great range of choice in wines. Along the way, at a picnic or a party, perhaps, or accompanying some steaming plate of pasta, a particular wine will taste absolutely marvelous. When this happens several times in a row we begin to get enthusiastic and want to find out more.

Everybody discovers the world of wines for himself. This book charts the wines of Europe, so that you can do your own exploring without detours and breakdowns.

One out of every five bottles of wine made in the world is white. Starting with the whites makes sense simply because there are fewer white wines to find out about, perhaps a couple of hundred. Since half of these are sweet, meant to be enjoyed by themselves or with dessert, the list is even further shortened because most people think of dry wines as table wines to accompany food. White table wines from the northern vineyards of France and the Rhineland have a fruity taste or a flowery taste, with a tartness not unlike that of a good apple or even a steely dryness. The short growing season builds up the fruit acids in the grapes without building up very much sugar to convert to alcohol when the grapes ferment. This makes these northern white wines light in alcoholic content yet hard, sometimes almost sharp.

Most people at first prefer the soft wines of the southern vineyards from around the Mediterranean. Many of these are also fruity or flowery. The longer, gentler growing season replaces more of the fruit acids with sugar.

All the white wines taste best chilled, making them

pleasant and familiar because we Americans are so used to cold drinks. For my own taste, these soft wines of Italy and southern France, of Spain and Portugal, are best when very cold, even with ice in them, the glass beaded with moisture, cool to the fingers when you sip. Nothing tastes so good on a hot summer day with cold seafood, or a hot casserole of shrimp or lobster or clams, with smoky hams or spicy sausages.

But now what about the red wines? The red wines of the south have that same gentle softness, while those of the north are hearty and full. Before exploring them, however, you might like to try some of the rosés, those pink wines made by pressing red grapes but letting the juice ferment only for a short time in contact with the skins, so that it picks up only a little color. Rosés are made in every wine district. They are best served cold and seem suited to the same dishes that go best with white wines. Rosés taste lighter and simpler than red wines. It is customary to serve them with almost any food—although roasts and chops and stews seem to call for the fuller red wines to either contrast with or complement the rich tastes of beef and fowl.

All table wines, white, red or rosé, are simply the fermented juice of freshly squeezed grapes. They are about 12 percent alcohol, never more than 14 percent, and about as strong as a well diluted highball.

Over the centuries, however, man has added all sorts of things to wine to vary the taste or change it completely.

Add bubbles and you get sparkling wine, the most famous, of course, being Champagne.

Add brandy, which is distilled wine, and you get Port or Sherry.

Add herbs and get fortified wine like Vermouth.

Add fruit flavoring or spices or barks and roots, and

you get aperitifs like Dubonnet. These popular wines, forerunners of the cocktail and highball, are very much back in fashion. There are all sorts of wine variations now: May Wine from the Rhineland, Sangria from Spain, modern versions of the wine punches our forefathers used to make.

All the kinds of wines are worth exploring. They are all made to appeal to certain kinds of dishes, particular times of day, special moods or memorable events. There are always new ones to be discovered— and so many different wines because there are so many ways to enjoy them. What may at first appear confusing turns out at last to be a delight, as those very differences become familiar and wines become a joy.

FRANCE

LOIRE
1 Muscadet
2 Anjou
3 Saumur
4 Bourgueil, Chinon
5 Vouvray
6 Pouilly-Fumé, Sancerre

RHÔNE
1 Côte Rôtie
2 Hermitage
3 Tavel
4 Châteauneuf-du-Pape

BURGUNDY
1 Chablis
2 Côte de Nuits
3 Côte de Beaune
4 Chalonnais
5 Maconnais
6 Beaujolais

BORDEAUX
1 Médoc
2 Pomerol
3 St. Émilion
4 Graves
5 Sauternes

LOIRE 5

FRANCE

BORDEAUX

RIOJA

VINHO VERDE

PORTUGAL

SPAIN

EUROPEAN WINE REGIONS

GERMANY

GERMANY

1 Mosel, Saar, Ruwer
2 Rheingau
3 Rheinhessen
4 Rheinpfalz
5 Franconia

SWITZERLAND

1 Neuchâtel
2 Vaud
3 Valais
4 Ticino

ITALY

1 PIEDMONT
  Barolo
2 LOMBARDY
  Valtellina
3 VENETO
  Soave, Bardolino,
  Valpolicella
4 EMILIA
  Lambrusco
5 TUSCANY
  Chianti
6 UMBRIA
  Orvieto, Est!Est!!Est!!!
7 THE MARCHES
  Verdicchio
8 LATIUM
  Frascati
9 CAMPANIA
  Lacryma Christi

HOW TO READ A WINE LABEL

A wine label is packed with information, short and cryptic, telling where the wine comes from, what kind of wine it is, and who has shipped it and imported it. The more specific the label, in general, the better the wine.

① BURGUNDY RED TABLE WINE indicates the general region and type. Note that the country of orgin is indicated and the quantity of wine contained in the bottle.

② CHASSAGNE-MONTRACHET and MORGEOT indicate 1) the township where the wine comes from; and 2) the actual vineyard. Note that if the wine were a Great Growth or First Growth, the phrases *Grand Cru* or *Premier Cru* would appear on the label.

③ APPELLATION CONTROLEE indicates that the place of origin—both township and vineyard—are protected by French law and that the wine meets the stringent requirements demanded by such laws. Note that the alcoholic content of the wine is given, although the phrase "table wine" is often considered to be enough and indicates that the wine is not more than 14% alcohol.

④ MIS EN BOUTEILLE PAR, plus the following phrases, indicates the wine is "put in bottle by" Joseph Drouhin, a firm founded in 1880, a shipper (Négociant) whose offices are in Beaune, the capital of Burgundy.

Note that when the owner of a vineyard bottles his own wines his name would be indicated as *Propriétaire* or *Récoltant* or *Viticulteur*, and the phrase, "*Mise au Domaine*" or a variant would appear on the label. Such wines are called estate-bottlings and are a further guarantee of authenticity but not of quality.

A confusing phrase often seen is "*Mis en bouteille dans nos caves*," "put in bottle in our cellars," which has no official meaning. It merely indicates that the shipper tended and bottled the wines rather than simply buying wines already in bottle and sticking his own label on it. This was common practice in the old days and the phrase lingers.

The importer is always indicated, usually at the bottom of the label or on a strip label placed just below.

The vintage may be indicated on the label, but it is often put on a separate neck label.

SOFT WHITE WINES
OF THE MEDITERRANEAN

Wines have always been magic. Soft and enchanting, they came to Europe out of the East, from Persia and beyond. They were the final triumph of the harvest, part of banquet and festival, a gift of the gods for the rites of spring but a simple boon, as well. Part of the daily fare that came from the wonder of fermentation, like bread and cheese, they tided the ancients over lean times with something more than sustenance. The Greeks scattered vineyards through their islands and colonies among the Roman tribes. The Phoenicians carried vines along the trade routes, planting them on the hilly coasts of the Riviera and all the way west to the mouth of the Rhone. For three thousand years the wines the world knew were the soft and changing vintages of the Mediterranean—the sea in the middle of the land.

The most desired of trade goods brought to wandering tribes, wines opened the way to empire. Roman conquerors planted vineyards on the frontiers—along the Danube and the Rhine, the Moselle and the Loire, the length of Spain and Portugal, even in southern

Britain. We know the same wines today, only they are better now.

The ancients preferred wines that were soft and sweet, hiding flaws by adding honey and herbs, cooling them with snow brought down from the mountains by runners. They had no choice, for wines too full of sugar ferment unevenly and go bad quickly. Most wines were drunk in the spring following the vintage. There were anxious moments as the great jars emptied, worry whether enough wine would stay good to last through the hot months of summer. Whites wines especially suffered from changes and those that didn't go bad were sought out. Wines from northern Italian hills became famous, their fruit acids keeping them fresh and pleasing into the second year, and even the third. Bacchus loved the hills, the Romans would say, and the styles they learned to like set the fashion for almost two thousand years.

Some wines from southern slopes were found to stay good with keeping, allowed to become golden, then gradually turning brown. The wealthy of the day came to prefer these, some of which were kept for decades. Even then, there were two kinds of wine —the fresh and pleasing wines of the last vintage, plentiful and inexpensive and good; the old and golden

The ancient wines were strange. As grapes mature, fruit acids are replaced by fruit sugars which convert to alcohol during fermentation. Too much sugar makes fermentation difficult to control, however, and off-tastes develop. Not until this century has enough been learned about fermentation so that some of the fruit acids are retained to give freshness to the wine.

wines full of strange tastes that had to be corrected with honey and spices.

Charlemagne extended the vineyards in the wake of the barbarians. Crusaders brought back new vines from the East. Monasteries raised the tending of vines from a craft to an art and learned to keep the wines in oaken casks so they would last longer. Burgundies, fresh and dry, that continued to improve with age, became the fashion, supplanting in favor the soft wines of the Mediterranean. To save their markets, the Italian vintners of the north began adopting the new techniques, establishing anew the fame of their wines, then bringing their methods and their vines to the new world of the Americas, North and South. Of all the soft white wines of the Mediterranean, those from Italy carried the old tradition to the modern world in the face of competition from those of the valleys of France and the Rhineland.

Other wines come from all around the Mediterranean and from its islands, and they are slowly beginning to appear on the market. One of the large producers is Greece—and you might look for the wines of Cambas.

ITALY

Wines gush from the slopes of every hill, it sometimes seems, the foothills of the Alps to the coastal slopes of Sicily, but the Italians drink more wine than anybody else, and the miracle may be that a few bottles get out of the country. However much they drink— some forty gallons per person every year—Italians are casual about wines, even nonchalant. Only in the past decade have they completed the control laws that describe the districts, protect the place names, and prescribe the methods of vine tending and wine mak-

ing. All this meticulous effort, completed after decades
so that the wines can move freely in the European
Economic Community, is summed up on the wine label
as D. O. C.—*Denominazione di Origine Controllata.*
This Controlled Denomination of Origin provides a
guarantee of authenticity patterned after the French
system of *Appellation Contrôlée.* The average Italian
ignores all this, of course, driving into the country to
seek out local wines from small growers. He even re-
sents the new laws because good wines of small districts
like Capri can now be exported.

Already, Italians are having trouble getting their
great white wines—Soave, from the hills around Verona,

Orvieto of Umbria, Verdicchio from the slopes running
down to the Adriatic, Frascati from the Roman hills.
Today these wines are drier, *secco,* than they used to
be. Still soft and flowery, they have a crispness, clean-
ness and a delicacy they never had before modern wine
making practices were adopted. They are the wines
people are apt to call charming or delicious when
served with seafood, fowl or lightly seasoned dishes.

Italians still hanker after sweet wines—*abboccato*—and that version of Orvieto is as popular as the dry. Most districts making dry whites also produce sweet versions, even letting the grapes dry somewhat to concentrate the sugar; modern wine making does away with off-tastes. Every district produces wines from Muscat grapes, often sweet, but the most famous is semi-sweet, called Est! Est!! Est!!!, from north of Rome. Wines from around Sicily's volcano, Etna, for instance, are made both dry and sweet, still or sparkling. Americans generally prefer the dry wines, finding them readily by watching out for the word *secco* on the label. Here is a list of distinctive white wines:

SOAVE   Perhaps the most distinguished of Italy's soft white wines, the name means suave, gentle, soft—a perfect description of the wine. Experts rank it the best white wine of Italy, perhaps mostly because it so typifies what a splendid white of the south should be. Those who discover they like it will also like the wines of the Loire and the soft whites from the Bordeaux district of Graves. Pale and fragrant, it is a perfect wine for a summer day or when you want to feel as if it were. The wine comes in tall, slim green bottles.

ORVIETO   This was the white companion for Chianti until that district began marketing so much of its own white wine. It has a character all its own, a fragrance like new-mown hay. Named after the ancient Etruscan city that dominates the district, it seems to reflect the aura of that ancient and mysterious people whose language is still unknown to us. Generally marketed in a squat straw-covered flask—a *fiasco* like those that so much Chianti is shipped in—it is available dry or sweet, *secco* or *abboccato*, words to look for on the label to be sure you are getting the one you want.

ITALIAN WHITE WINE

Verdicchio Classico
dei Castelli di Jesi

DENOMINAZIONE DI ORIGINE CONTROLLATA
PRODOTTO E IMBOTTIGLIATO ALL'ORIGINE NELLA
CANTINA SOCIALE DI CUPRAMONTANA
COOP. r.l.
CUPRAMONTANA (ANCONA)
PRODUCT   OF ITALY
NET CONTENTS 1 PT. 8 FL. OZ.   ALCOHOL 12% BY VOLUME

SOLE AGENT *Dreyfus, Ashby & Co.* NEW YORK N.Y.

VERDICCHIO   Named for the grape from which
it is made, Verdicchio is a delicate wine with a light
taste of the earth in which it is grown, and a fresh
quality best described as crispness. It is the sort of
wine you feel you ought to drink in a leafy arbor or
on a terrace by the sea. Like all the white and soft dry
wines of Italy, Verdicchio will somehow remind you
of summer, of spring.

The soft wines of Italy are drier and fresher than
they used to be, particularly the Verdicchio from
Castelli di Jesi and those from the Verdiso grape
planted around Conegliano, north of Venice.
A sweet version of Verdiso is called Prosecco.

EST! EST!! EST!!!   The old story goes that a wine-loving Bishop on his way to Rome sent a man ahead to seek out the good wines, chalking on the walls *Est*, the current Italian slang for "here it is." In a town called Flask Mountain—Montefiascone—the scout was carried away. He wrote Est! Est!! Est!!! It's almost impossible to drink the wine without being told the story at least three times. The wine is softly sweet, or half-sweet, depending on how you would like to describe it, and is particularly good with mild cheeses and fruit, or with dishes made with fruit.

FRASCATI   This, the favorite white wine of Rome, comes from Castelli Romani, the hills where the nobility constructed their villas. The wine is drunk everywhere in the city, its fresh and fruity taste epitomizing Roman gusto.

CORTESE   A white wine grape of the Piedmont, the northern province bordering France that produces some of the most distinguished of Italian wines. The Cortese produced around Alessandria is light, flowery and dry, meant to be drunk young. Fuller versions from the Riviera vineyards to the south, in the province of Liguria, are wines for hearty fish stews, while a semi-sweet version from Gavi might be served with creamed seafood or fruit. The fragrant and elegant Cortese from Alessandria is best with simply cooked fish and fowl.

CHIANTI BIANCO   White Chianti, companion of the famous red, has always been made, but until recently little has been exported. A straw-colored wine, full of taste and fragrance, it is made primarily from the Trebbiano, which gives it a distinctive taste. It is best drunk young.

FRANCE
WHITE BORDEAUX

Although Bordeaux is famous first for red wines, many more whites come from this region. Once a Roman colony and vacation spot, its first wines were fashioned for Roman tastes, soft and straw-tasting young wines and luscious golden old ones. Until the days of Queen Elizabeth, wines shipped from the port of Bordeaux were known as Graves, which means gravel.

Wines from the gravelly vineyards were so popular that vineyards all around them were planted in the same grapes to make the same soft wine. Most of these are now marketed as Bordeaux Blanc for the lightest and Bordeaux Blanc Supérieur for somewhat fuller wines. Minimum alcoholic content determines classification. Changing tastes and modern methods have influenced growers to make ever-drier wines, and these are marketed under the old names. Those called Graves are considered the best. Many of the new dry whites, are now marketed as Blanc de Blancs, a name borrowed from Champagne producers meaning that it is a white wine from white grapes. The word *sec*, meaning dry, also appears on labels.

As attention switched to the reds of Bordeaux, Graves and its kindred fell from favor. They are still almost unknown to the present generation, so there is plenty of wine to meet demand and prices are low. Graves and the other white Bordeaux are among the best buys in the world of wines today. Try those of Schröder and Schÿler, founded in 1702.

This decade will see a change. Along the Loire, the Bordeaux grapes like Sauvignon Blanc and Sémillon make distinctive wines, ranging from dry to flowery to fruity. As the public discovers that the same sort of wines occur in Bordeaux, they will be sought after. Already, wines identified with the grape names are beginning to appear on the market. Some of the little-known white wine districts are beginning to market wines under their own names, and soon to become familiar are Entre-Deux-Mers, Premières-Côtes-de-Bordeaux, Sainte Croix-du-Mont.

VOUVRAY   The white wine from the Touraine typifies for me the essential nature of Mediterranean wines, although the vineyards along the Loire are a long way from the sea. It varies widely from vintage to vintage and always tastes good. A century ago it was mostly a soft wine, on the dry side in poor years and short-lived, on the sweet side in good years and good for a decade. It can be made fruity and dry in years no better than "fair," marvelous with fish and fowl. But in great years, it is sweet and luscious, lighter and less rich than Sauternes, a wine that can last for twenty years. In poor years it is pale and fresh, even sometimes slightly sparkling, or *pétillant*. When this tendency is developed, Vouvray can be a delicious sparkling wine. It is the most interesting wine made from the Chenin Blanc grape, one to go back to every few months just to see what it's like.

SAUMUR   Downstream from Vouvray is Anjou and the large district of Saumur, whose wines resemble those of its neighbor. Much of the whites are made into soft sparkling wines. Richer whites, also from the Chenin Blanc, are made in the small Anjou district to the west, Coteaux du Layon. Saumur produces reds and rosés from the Cabernet Franc. The best red is Champigny, overshadowed only by Chinon and Saint Nicholas, whose vineyards lie to the east, across the border in Touraine. In Anjou, also, are Coteaux de l'Aubance, known for its rosés Coteaux du Loir, known for white Jasnières, and Coteaux de la Loire, known for fruity white Savennières. The best way to enjoy them is to open a bottle of Saumur, white, rosé or red, then try one of the others. There is scarcely a better way to see how wines from a particular grape can vary, even when planted only a few miles apart.

PORTUGAL

The wines of Portugal are what they are today strictly because of foreign influences—Roman legions, two English brothers and some Americans. Romans planted the vineyards, so delighting the Portuguese that they have continued to extend them for two thousand years, drinking most of the wine themselves.

And then, after three centuries of occupation, the French kicked the English out of Bordeaux in 1453.

Loss of their wine-producing colony so angered the British that they slapped exorbitant duties on French wines, cutting off their tongues to spite their palates, so to speak. Glumly, they supped with low-duty wines from Spain and Portugal, but it wasn't the same thing. Two lads sent out from London to scour Portugal for something more palatable stopped overnight at a monastery and were served a delicious red wine, strong and sweet, made by stopping the fermentation with a dose of brandy. They called it Porto because it was shipped from Oporto and it became the rage of London.

The Portuguese were pleased to have the new revenue, content to drink the broad range of table wines. Nothing much changed for five hundred years until new wines were needed for the American market. Just the thing was found in Portugal.

Importers had been watching the growing popularity of Portuguese table wines. These were practically unknown in America. After a few tasting trips, the importers found just what they wanted.

From the north they found a wine of an estate that dated back to the 17th century, a fresh pink wine in a squat round bottle, Mateus. Just south was the district of Dão, long known for red wines, where they found the lusty Grão Vasco. And just north they found the Vinho Verde from the old estate of Aveleda, producers of Casal Garcia.

Vinho verde means green wine in Portuguese. This doesn't refer to its color but to the fact that it is bottled young and should be drunk young. The wine is the pet of the Portuguese, red, rosé or white, but the pale, soft straw-colored white is the one preferred. The wine from Aveleda is the most popular one in Portugal. The vineyards were replanted with French

vines over a century ago by the Guedes family, and it has become the largest vineyard holding in the country. French techniques proved so popular that they were extended to the Mateus vineyards and to the Dão estates. It was this combined group of wines that was introduced to the United States. It was successful. A decade later the American popularity of Mateus made it the largest selling wine in the world, with Casal Garcia and Grão Vasco following right along. The Portuguese are of two minds, enjoying the limelight, but wondering if foreign demand for *vinho verde* may not limit the amount of wine available at home.

SPAIN

The Spanish history is much like that of Portugal, their most popular wine being the Sherry from Jerez. With a difference. The Spanish have always drunk much of their own Sherries, particularly the dry types, while the sweet ones were popular abroad. Like Portugal, though, until recently Spanish table wines were strictly for home consumption. Some wines of the northern region of Rioja found foreign markets, but other vineyards around Barcelona and from Valdepenas in the south were rarely exported. So far this century the fashion has been for French and German

and Italian wines, but modern methods have so improved Spanish vintages they demand attention.

Wine making in Spain had changed little since the Romans, until disaster struck the vineyards just before the turn of the century. American vines were introduced to Europe by enterprising scientists who knew even less about ecology than we do today. On the vine roots was a burrowing louse called *phylloxera*, which devastated all European vineyards. The French discovered ways to graft European vines to resistant American roots and the technique was adopted all over Europe. Early in the devastation, however, many French wine-making families emigrated to Spain and elsewhere, introducing first their methods and then their grapes.

By the middle of this century, when secrets of fermentation were discovered to further improve wines, visitors to Spain began discovering unexpected excellencies in the northern vineyards. Then came the New York World's Fair. The smash hit of the fair was the Spanish Pavilion.

The Spanish are as nonchalant about wines as the Italians, and a favorite hot weather drink is a bottle of wine poured in a pitcher, to which is added the juice of a lemon and the juice of an orange, with ice and maybe a little sugar. It's called Sangria and a glass or two is a fine way to beat the heat. New York summers during the Fair were hot, and practically every visitor discovered Sangria in the elegant restaurants of the Pavilion, served with the fish and seafood flown in daily from Spain. Visitors also discovered the silvery-gold white wines, with tastes faintly reminiscent of hay stacked in sunny fields, or mossy mountain glens. They went home, remembering the wines as much as they remembered the Pavilion. Spanish table wines began to take their places in the shops beside those from other parts of Europe.

RIOJA   The vineyards lie in foothills west of Barcelona in nothern Spain, planted in French grape varieties and Spanish vines that have proved their worth over the centuries. The whites have a softness that is combined with a certain crispness, giving them a distinctive taste that seems particularly suited to fish and seafood. They are, somehow, warm-weather wines for drinking with cold foods—salads and sandwiches and the like—but their special tastes also seem just right with casseroles and rice dishes like paella.

DRY WINES
OF THE SLOPES

The further north you go the drier wines become, for vineyards need much warm sun to plump the grapes. Some vines thrive at the struggle to get enough sun, to build enough sugar in the grapes to make fermentation possible without excess sugar, which would add sweetness. The best dry wines come from hillside vineyards where the angle catches the sun more directly. These are the most popular wines of all.

The greatest dry white wines come from the slopes of Burgundy, where the Chardonnay grape is used to make astounding wines. Crisp dry wines come from hills above the Loire planted in Chenin Blanc. In Swiss valleys shaded by mountains, other grapes are used because the Chardonnay and Chenin Blanc won't ripen; the wines are equally dry but lighter in taste and in alcohol. Along the Rhine, more quickly-maturing grapes are needed, all of them with a special flowery taste that lessens the sensation of dryness; these come from the Riesling grape or the Sylvaner.

For noble dry whites then, go first to Burgundy, and when you get there, start with the driest—Chablis.

Chablis itself lies north of the Côte d'Or, which is

the main part of Burgundy. All its greatest vineyards are on a single hillside. These vineyards are called "Great Growths," *Grands Crus*, and produce perhaps 12,000 cases of wine in a good year.

Fortunately, there are some 700 acres of neighboring vineyards, not much more than a square mile, that produce wines only slightly less grand. They are called *Premiers Crus*—First Growths—and may produce 100,000 cases in a good year. Other vineyards are entitled to sell their wines simply as "Chablis," and still others on more distant hills mark their wines "Petit Chablis." All in all, perhaps a couple of hundred thousand cases are produced in Chablis in a good year. The same scarcity exists with all great wines.

To buy a Great Growth or First Growth, all you need to look for on a label is *"Grand Cru"* or *"Premier Cru,"* accompanied by the words *"Appelation Contrôlée,"* which means the wine conforms to the control laws. More detail—the vineyard and vintage, the shipper and sometimes the grower—will appear on the label, but the above phrases are enough to identify the

There are only seven Chablis vineyards, totaling less than a hundred acres, and their names are known to wine lovers around the world: Vaudesir, Les Clos, Les Preuses, Grenouilles, Valmur, Blanchots, Bougros. Portions of two of them form a five-acre plot producing wine that has long been sold as Moutonne. The vineyards are parceled among several owners, who may make a little cask of wine from one section, called a *feuillette*, or a still smaller cask from another, called a *quartaut*. A *quartaut* holds less than a hundred bottles of wine, half as many as the *feuillette*.

great wines. Similar phrases identify the top wines of Bordeaux and the Rhine. In Burgundy look for such shippers as Drouhin and Bichot.

The greatest dry white wines of Burgundy, fuller and rounder than Chablis, come from the Côte d'Or, the Golden Slope that is the heart of the region. The whites are concentrated in its southern half, a length of hillside scarcely a dozen miles long that is named after its principal town, the Côte de Beaune. At one end is the vineyard of Corton-Charlemagne, at the other are those of Montrachet, and in the middle are those of Meursault. The wines are unequaled anywhere.

Vineyards neighboring those of world fame may produce glorious wines available at half the price, wines to buy the nine times out of ten when you feel you can't afford the Cortons of the world. The two towns, Ladoix and Pernand, have more than a square mile of vineyards between them in addition to Corton; Aloxe-Corton has more. There's another square mile of vineyard in neighboring Savigny, and more in the hamlets of Chorey-les-Beaune and Saint Aubin. Whites from such towns are usually blended together, to be marketed as "Côte de Beaune," with the name of the

town shown on the label. They are wines to look for
when you can't buy Corton.

Corton-Charlemagne is the fullest of white Burgundies, matched in fame only by the Montrachets
from the southern end of the district. Montrachet is
said to be somehow grander, with a fuller bouquet.
But this is wine talk. Drinking either one is a unique
experience. Few of us get to taste the wines, for there
are a scant 10,000 cases of Corton-Charlemagne and
even less Montrachet. There are several vineyards
entitled to the latter name: Le Montrachet, itself, Che-
valier-Montrachet, Bâtard-Montrachet, Bienvenues-Bâ-

Corton-Charlemagne is said to have been planted
by the emperor who welded together the Holy
Roman Empire. He ordered the planting of many
vineyards—among them the most famous on the
Rhine, Schloss Johannisberg—with the idea that
trade in wines would unite the people of Europe.
The man had vision. A thousand years have
passed. Finally in 1970, an overall wine law for
the European Economic Community was put in
force, and wines are beginning to pass freely
between its members.

Corton-Charlemagne is better than ever. Its
vineyard extends beyond the township of
Aloxe-Corton, which has adopted the name as
part of its own as if to proclaim possession. But
the vineyard extends into the adjoining communes
of Ladoix and Pernand-Vergelesses. A fact of
surpassing unimportance? Much more than
anyone wants to know about a wine? Not when
you're putting up eight dollars a bottle.

Joseph Drouhin

PRODUCE OF FRANCE
WHITE BURGUNDY TABLE WINE

CONTENTS : 1 PINT 8 FL. OZS
ALCOHOL BY VOLUME 12°5

Montrachet

APPELLATION CONTROLÉE

Marquis de Laguiche

MONOPOLE : JOSEPH DROUHIN, NÉGOCIANT A BEAUNE, COTE-D'OR

Dreyfus Ashby & Co

tard-Montrachet and Criots-Bâtard-Montrachet. All of them are *Grands Crus*.

The *Grands Crus* of Montrachet also come from the adjoining communes of Puligny and Chassagne, which are entitled to add that famous name to their own. Other vineyards in the town are entitled to be labeled *"Premier Cru."* Wines bearing the town names Puligny-Montrachet and Chassagne-Montrachet, and not the name of a vineyard, may be good. But they should by no means be confused with the great vineyard wines.

Between Corton and Montrachet is the township of Meursault, whose wines are considered to be softer than the others. The best of the vineyards are entitled to add the phrase, *Premier Cru*, to their labels. A little white wine comes from other famous townships of the Golden Slope, notably, Beaune itself, Chambolle-Musigny and Clos de Vougeot, but these wines are rarely seen.

There are wines from two townships in the Côte Chalonnaise just south of the Golden Slope that can occasionally be found, Montagny and Rully. But the white Burgundy everybody knows is Pouilly-Fuissé.

Its fame may be due to the fact that the name is hard to pronounce, but, once mastered, easy to remember. It is, approximately, "pwee-yee fwee-say."

Pouilly-Fuissé is a large district in the Côte Maconnaise that produces something like a quarter of a million cases of full, dry white wine in a good year. Demand for it has sent its prices up until they match those of the much rarer Chablis, but the fact remains that this is a white Burgundy that can be found in most shops and on most restaurant wine lists. (Neighboring vineyards in the hamlets of Pouilly-Vinzelles

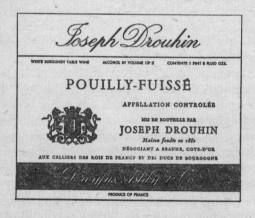

and Pouilly-Loché produce similar wines, and usually they are less expensive.

Much lower in price and made from the same grape, are other whites from the district marketed as Macon Blanc Supérieur, or Macon Blanc. Like all the great Burgundies, they are made from the Chardonnay grape and can be called Pinot Chardonnay Macon. Another grape, called the Aligoté, goes to market as Bourgogne

Blanc. When blended with Chardonnay, it is often labeled, Blanc de Blancs.

So many names, however logical, have hurt the marketing of white Burgundy. The *Grands Crus* and the *Premiers Crus* are very special wines and very rare, in the class with Rolls Royces and Bentleys. Explanations as to what they are become necessary because they are so superior to wines bearing only township names, like Puligny-Montrachet. But these township wines are generally excellent, as are district wines like Pouilly-Fuissé.

Bored with the explanations, people jump to the conclusion that Pinot Chardonnay Macon, Aligoté or Blanc de Blancs are scarcely worth bothering about. But these, too, are generally good buys, perhaps better values, because their prices are not inflated by fame or scarcity.

VINEYARD WINES

The town name plus a vineyard name, or *"Premier Cru"* accompanied by a town or vineyard name, or *"Grand Cru"* with or without the town name—what a lot of wines to choose from! Most people like them all. Chablis is considered to be particularly good with oysters or fish or shellfish when simply prepared. With rich sauces or ones not too highly seasoned, fish or seafood is generally matched with the Cortons and Montrachets. Such wines are also good with simply cooked fowl, as is Meursault. Ham and other spicy or smoked meats or dishes taste especially good with Pouilly-Fuissé and the Macons.

Anyone who gets to like the dry white Burgundies ought to explore each of the categories. On the next page there's a checklist to guide you.

REGIONAL WINES

> Bourgogne Blanc
> Bourgogne Aligoté or
>   Blanc de Blancs

DISTRICT & TOWNSHIP WINES

> Pinot Chardonnay Macon
> Macon Blanc
> Macon Blanc Supérieur
> Macon-Villages or St. Verand
> Pouilly-Fuissé, Pouilly-Vinzelles
>   or Pouilly-Loché
> Montagny or Rully
> Chassagne-Montrachet or
>   Puligny-Montrachet
> Meursault
> Aloxe-Corton

THE LOIRE

The Loire is the longest river of France and a bewildering range of wines comes from vineyards all along its western course. But most people think of them as soft and flowery country wines meant to be drunk at a picnic or a light lunch. This may once have been so, but, like the white wines of Italy, modern methods have widened the range from extremely dry Muscadet to the flowery dry Pouilly-Fumé to the often-sweet and always fragrant Vouvray. Traditionally, the wines were so light and meant to be drunk so young that they were not supposed to travel. It was

Michel Dreyfus who realized that these improvements made the wines excellent choices for Americans.

Dreyfus was a wine buyer in the grand tradition, always on the lookout for good wines not known to the market and conscious that the great fame of the noted vineyards of Burgundy and Bordeaux meant inflated prices. A native of Switzerland, he had traveled the Continent for thirty years, working with the wine staffs of hotels and restaurants before coming to this country just before the New York World's Fair of 1939. Many old friends ran pavilions at the fair and many decided to stay and open restaurants. Their presence inspired a renaissance of fine dining in New York, and Dreyfus helped them get good wines. The splendid restaurants were perfect places to introduce new bottlings, the first of which was Pouilly-Fumé.

The vineyards had been planted by the Romans, but in the Middle Ages monks came from Bordeaux with vines of the Sauternes district, the Sauvignon. The resulting wine had a remarkable freshness and was beautifully dry. It became a favorite of the French court, which summered in the great châteaux built along the lovely river. The Loire is called the smile of France, and Pouilly-Fumé seems to be its essence.

The wine was a hit in New York and Dreyfus turned his attention to the wine at the other end of the Loire, Muscadet, from a district near the river's mouth. Muscadet needs to be drunk young, its dry lightness losing freshness after a couple of years. It was a wine that had the reputation of not traveling well, but what this really meant was that it was a wine that could not be imported and then be allowed to languish on the shelf for years. Made from a Burgundy grape, the Melon, it developed a special and pleasing firmness in the vineyards near the Atlantic that made it a good companion for oysters, shellfish and shad of the Loire.

The result of these efforts was the beginning of a wider interest in wines by Americans who suddenly felt free of the tyranny of famous names and began to look for wines they didn't know much about. Continuing discovery is one of the excitements of wine.

As a consequence, other importers began bringing in Pouilly-Fumé and wines from neighboring districts like Sancerre and Quincy, soon followed by Muscadet.

These have in turn become famous, paving the way for discoveries from tiny districts like Pouilly-sur-Loire and Reuilly.

The most famous wine of the Loire is Vouvray, and even it is not typical of soft wines. For one thing, Vouvrays are quite sweet in good years when the growing season is long and much sugar builds up in the grapes. For another, a Vouvray often continues to improve for a decade, and even longer. It is made from a grape called the Chenin Blanc, whose wines are called by the grape name when they are dry. Vouvray is the fruitiest wine of the Loire and the fullest—the wine to drink when you want to begin exploring sweet wines.

POUILLY-FUME   Not really hard to pronounce, "pwee-yee foo-may," the name is supposed to come

de Ladoucette
Pouilly-Fumé

APPELLATION POUILLY-FUMÉ CONTROLÉE
DE LADOUCETTE FRÈRES
AU CHATEAU DU NOZET, POUILLY-SUR-LOIRE (NIÈVRE)
MISE EN BOUTEILLES DANS NOS CAVES

ALCOHOL 13%, BY VOLUME   STILL WHITE WINE
CONTENTS 1 PT. 8 FL. OZ.   PRODUCT OF FRANCE

SOLE   *Dreyfus, Ashby & Co.*   NEW YORK
AGENTS   N.Y.

from the fact that the vineyards are often clouded in mist that looks like smoke. The particular bottling introduced almost a generation ago is produced at the Château de Nozet by the fifth generation of the family and is called Ladoucette, which means a sweet young thing. The wine is just like a pretty girl. Feminine qualities are often used to describe the gentle wines of the Loire; half-bottles are called *fillettes*, little girls.

MUSCADET   Fresh, young, dry Muscadet is produced in several townships, the most distinguished
being Muscadet de Sèvre et Maine, from the south
bank of the river. The best bottlings come from individual proprietors like M. Sautejeau, the wine introduced by Dreyfus Ashby. The wine sometimes develops a slight sparkle called *pétillant* in French, which
beads the glass and adds to the sprightly taste.

It is customary these days to crush white wine
grapes and ferment the juice away from the skins, a
method that makes for lightness in the resulting wine.
Some Muscadet is fermented *sur lie*, on the skins, and
these fuller wines are so identified on the label.

SWITZERLAND

Surrounded on all sides by wine country, Switzerland has 30,000 vineyard acres of its own along the lake shores and river valleys that lead to them. Among the lightest and driest wines that can be found, the best come from the districts of the Vaud along Lake Geneva's north shore, still more from the shores of Neu-

châtel. The Valais, where the Rhone flows west into Lake Geneva before rushing into France, is the largest district. Most of the wines are made from the grape called the Fendant, and marketed as such, although some bear township names—Dézalay, Aigle, Saint Saphorin, Yvorne. Even the names are delicious.

NEUCHATEL   This Swiss wine is most familiar to Americans. Fresh-tasting because it is bottled the spring after the vintage when scarcely six months old, it is a wine that often shows beads of bubbles in the glass after it has been poured. The beading is called "the star" in Neuchâtel, the more of it the better, and

Vines were brought in over the mountain passes centuries ago, Riesling from the Rhineland, Pinot Noir and Chardonnay from Burgundy. These vines flourish, but the Chasselas of the Loire bears more grapes in the high valleys among the Alps and has become the favorite; it has even acquired a new name, Fendant, perhaps because it is the preferred wine to drink with cheese fondue.

seems to add a sprightliness to the taste as well as to the looks of the wine. (A pale and fruity red from the town of Cortaillod, made from the Pinot Noir, is one of two red wines that can occasionally be found in Switzerland; the other and better red is Dôle de Sion, from the Valais.)

VAUD   The main districts of this canton flank Lausanne, La Côte on the west, Lavaux on the east. The best wines come from Yvorne and Aigle in Chablais, the district at the eastern end of Lake Geneva, where vineyards extend up the Rhone. They are the fullest whites, marketed under both district and town names, the wines to drink with veal and fowl and cheese dishes that the Swiss make so simply and so well. Fish freshly caught in the lakes never tastes better than with these wines, dry as white Burgundies and crisp as those from the Loire, but sprightlier than either because they have been bottled so promptly after the vintage.

VALAIS   Palm trees grow in this valley of the Rhone, an almost tropic climate protected by the highest Alps. Vineyards extend from the foot of Mont Blanc at Martigny almost to the Simplon pass, to the towns of Visp and Sierre, whose vineyards are the world's highest, and whose wines seem to be the world's lightest. (Good reds from vineyards around Sion are called Dôle and are surprisingly full-bodied.) In recent years, there has been much experimentation with many of the noble grapes and some of these marketed with their grape names occasionally get by the thirsty Swiss. The area produces mostly light whites from the Fendant on nearly 10,000 acres of vineyard. Only shops with extensive wine selections are likely to stock them; distinctive wines are worth looking for.

FLOWERY WINES
OF THE RHINELAND

ALSACE:

Sylvaner
Traminer
Gewürztraminer
Tokay d'Alsace
Riesling

GERMANY:

Rheinpfalz
Rheinhessen
Rheingau
Mosel-Saar-Ruwer

Wines of the northern rivers are flowery, just as hillside wines are dry and wines of the south are soft, but the range is wide for all three. Rhineland wines are mostly from a single grape, the Riesling, tended much the same way and similarly vinified, and yet no grape offers such splendid variation. Like the color, which can range from a white close to crystal to a faint green tint, through silver and yellows to the deepest gold, so the smell ranges from a spicy hint of mountain flowers to the scent-filled richness of a summer garden. Taste can go from a ghostly trace that has been best defined as glorious water to a fruity tang almost of syrup that lasts for minutes after you have swallowed a sip. Some have the essence of spring, some the fullness of summer, others the richness of autumn. Drinking them is something like watching the Rhine, never the same, never changing, always different.

There's no good explaining. You simply have to taste the wines. And no matter how many of them you get to drink, there are always other wines to try, new vintages and old. The same is so for the dry wines of Burgundy and the Loire and Switzerland. There is an even wider range of all southern wines, because so many different grapes are used, planted in so many different soils. But their variety is nothing compared to the Rieslings of the Rhine.

A family of wines numbering in the hundreds, Rieslings have been bewildering to buy because the labeling was complicated—until the Alsatians decided to market their wines under grape names. The least of these wines was not the Riesling but the Sylvaner, a light

Vin d'Alsace

DEPUIS   1639

SYLVANER "HUGEL"
ESTATE BOTTLED
MARQUE DÉPOSÉE
F.E. HUGEL ET FILS NÉGOCIANTS A RIQUEWIHR (H⁺-RHIN)

SOLE AGENTS : DREYFUS, ASHBY & C⁰,
NEW-YORK N. Y.
ALCOHOL BY VOL : 12 % - NET CONTENTS : 1 PINT 8 FL. OZ.

and satisfying flowery wine. It is the most popular white of France, not only because it is cheap, but because it is just plain good. Americans, no longer awed by wine, are drinking more and more of it—when a cool glass of white wine tastes better than anything. Try one of those from the fine old firm of Hugel founded in 1639.

Also in the vineyards was Traminer, a grape whose wine has a particularly flowery, almost spicy taste. Many people think it is the best wine of Alsace. Special strains have been developed called Gewürztraminer, even more spicy, fuller, more flowery. This is a wine of such intensity that it is almost always best drunk by itself, or with a highly flavored fish or chicken dish. It is especially good with Oriental dishes. There is a particularly fruity wine made from the Pinot Gris called Tokay d'Alsace, because old bottles seemed reminiscent of the tonic Tokay of Hungary. All these wines are marketed under the grape names, so that they won't be confused with the Riesling.

The Sylvaner is grown extensively in the German region bordering Alsace, the Rheinpfalz, and in the region just to the north, Rheinhessen. Much of the wine is used for blends. The Riesling predominates in all the best vineyards, as it does in the Rheingau and the Moselle, the two most celebrated Rhineland regions. So that the wines could move freely within the European Community, the labeling has been greatly simplified.

ALSACE

The best wines come from the central section of the region, from north of Colmar to Selestat, called the Haut-Rhin. The towns are some of the most picturesque in Europe, full of tourists in the summer, but worth a visit for all that because the inns and restaurants are so good. There is trout from the mountain streams, sausages and hams and cheeses, chicken and ducks and geese, not to mention the *foie gras* of Strasbourg. Sauerkraut becomes almost a delicacy in Alsace, chicken and duck often cooked in wine on a bed of it, but the favorite of all is *choucroute garnie*, the sauerkraut simmered in wine of the countryside with smoked ham and pork chops, various sausages, potatoes, carrots, peppercorns and juniper berries for spiciness. Nothing tastes better with Sylvaner. Or Traminer. Or Gewürztraminer. Or Riesling. These are the best known wine towns:

Ammerschwir	Kaysersberg
Mittelwihr	Riquewihr
Kientzheim	Ribeauvillé
	Bergheim

GERMANY

Innocents used to take one look at a German wine label, then take another, because they couldn't believe their eyes. If French wines were confusing, German labels were even more detailed. All the best wines were made from the Riesling, but there were thousands of different names and phrases. Today, to move freely in the Common Market, the names have been simplified.

• To get the top grades of dry wines today, the word to look for on a label is *Kabinett*.

• Wines more flowery and fruity are labeled *Spätlese*.

• Wines more fruity than flowery are labeled *Auslese*.

There's a story of how these special late-picked grapes came to be used for wines. The date when the vintage begins is always set by local ordinance, and in the old days this was the province of the Bishop of Fulda. When the grapes were ripe, he sent a messenger to inform the town fathers, but the messenger was waylaid. The anxious town fathers sent a query to the bishop, who sent another messenger, who was again waylaid. It was now well into October, and the town fathers again petitioned the bishop. This time, the messenger got through, but the grapes had dried on the vines, some of them shriveled to raisins. Despairing, they made the wines anyway, separating the bunches and the berries according to ripeness. When the wine was made, one was more luscious than the other—and that's how the practice began.

At the turn of the century when sweet wines were the rage, too many grapes were left to make the specialized wines. Today, the *Trockenbeerenauslesen* and *Beerenauslesen* are so expensive that many more grapes are picked at full ripeness to make *Kabinett* wines, and only in exceptional years are there many *Spätlesen* and *Auslesen*.

The Rhineland is so far north—the same latitude as Labrador—that in poor years grapes may not ripen fully. When they fail to do so, sugar is added to the fermenting juice so that the wine will have enough alcohol, about 10%, to keep it from spoiling. These sugared wines—not really sweet because all of the sugar has been converted to alcohol—are the ones identified as "*Tafelwein*" or "*Qualitätswein*" on labels. The process is called *chaptalization* and is customary in all northern vineyards. Wines officially ranked as *Kabinett* have no such additions, the alcohol coming only from the natural sugar in the grapes. This is also true of wines labeled *Qualitätswein mit Prädikat*.

There are other grades above and below *Kabinett*, *Spätlese* and *Auslese* and they might as well be spelled out.

What's called *Tafelwein* is common wine, ordinary table wine meant to be drunk within a few months of the vintage. The grade called Quality Wine, *Qualitätswein*, is meant to be drunk up before the following vintage. Better than table wine, some of them may be used in the cheapest grades of wines with brand names. Not much of this will get beyond the cafés and bistros of Europe. The ones being shipped abroad fall into the category called *Qualitätswein mit Prädikat*, a phrase that appears on the label. This means, roughly, a quality wine with special rank or title, one that can live at least a year or two after the vintage, improving in bottle. The phrase categorizes the special way that grapes are picked in the Rhineland vineyards.

The ripe grapes are made into dry and flowery wines that are rarely much above 11% in alcohol. These are *Kabinett* wines. Many bunches are left on the vines to ripen still more and are picked late; these become *Spätlesen*, still dry but more fruity than flowery. Particularly ripe bunches from the late-picking are separated and made into still fruitier wines called *Auslesen*, harvest selections. In great years, individual grapes are selected from the over-ripe bunches for *Beerenauslesen*, and even more dried-up or raisinized berries are sorted out and made into *Trockenbeerenauslesen*. Both these wines are sweet, rare and expensive, meant for drinking by themselves or with desserts.

People who like dry wines can fall in love with those called *Kabinett*. They have a sprightly dry taste that reminds you of daffodils and apple blossoms and new grass. And it's quite true that the *Spätlesen* taste of summer, while the *Auslesen* taste of autumn. Each bottle is a surprise. Don't miss the bottlings of Louis Guntrum and those of Valkenberg.

Maybe the best way to get an idea of these wines is to go to Rüdesheim in the Rheingau in the height of the tourist season and spend an evening in the Drösselgasse, Thrush Alley. The little street is lined with wine taverns and students flock there from all over Europe. There's a German band, complete with accordion and tuba, playing oom-pah-pah. Girls in dirndls rush around setting long, slim bottles on the big tables. You sit down anywhere you can find a seat, crowding in with others at the table, a little uneasy at the noise and bustle.

You order a bottle of wine, deciding to watch the fun for a while. The band starts to play and everybody starts to sing, linking arms and swaying to the music. You hum along, tapping out the time, less uneasy now because you see everybody is having a good time. What, the wine's gone already? Well, let's order another bottle and then we'll go. Suddenly, somebody links arms with you and you find yourself singing. You begin to learn some of the words. Several bottles and several hours later, you may be able to tear yourself away, and head out into the street for your hotel. Chances are you're still singing. People have been doing so for hundreds of years.

You needn't take a trip, of course, to find out about the wines. Buy half a dozen bottles of *Kabinett*, different ones, of course, and invite some friends over. The list that follows, naming the main townships in the various regions, will enable you to choose wines.

RHEINPFALZ   The Pfalz borders Alsace and is also known as the Palatinate. Wines come from more than 30,000 acres which were once the main source of vintages for the Holy Roman Empire. Full-bodied and fruity, they are the wines for picnics, buffets and party dishes like casseroles. The best come from:

> Ruppertsberg
> Deidesheim
> Forst
> Wachenheim

German wines of the better grades carry the name of the town with *er* added on, the way a resident of New York is called a New Yorker; a vineyard name is added to further identify the wine. A Forster Mariengarten comes from the vineyard of Mariengarten in Forst township; the vineyard is made up of parcels that once had various names, all of which are now sold as Mariengarten.

Before the new laws, every township had scores of vineyards. Some were only an acre, or even less. Now, the minimum size for Rhineland vineyards has been set at a little more than twelve acres, so that smaller parcels are lumped together under a single name, a *Grosslage*. Wines from these small parcels may be blended and sold under the generic name. However, individual growers may decide to bottle wines from their own parcels separately. This will be indicated on the label by the words "Aus eigenem Lesegut" or "Eigene Abfüllung," meaning from his own vintage or his own bottling, indicating estate-bottling.

RHEINHESSEN   Hessia is the region just above the Pfalz, containing about as many vineyard acres, much of which is planted in Sylvaner. It is the original home of Liebfraumilch, all of which once came from a small vineyard beside the cathedral in Worms. Liebfraumilch is now a blend of wines from all over the region, and even includes wines from the Pfalz and elsewhere, quality depending entirely on what the shipper chooses to put in his blend; in most cases, the

German wines are traditionally sold in tall slim bottles made of brown glass for wines of the Rheingau and Rheinhessen and green glass for the Moselle and Rheinpfalz.

higher the price, the better the Liebfraumilch, which can be excellent.

The best vineyards are planted in the Riesling, generally, the wines having a full bouquet and a fruity taste. The following towns have the reputation for producing the best wines:

Oppenheim
Nierstein
Nackenheim
Bingen

RHEINGAU   The north-flowing Rhine crooks west at Mainz for twenty miles, bending north again near Rüdesheim. The short stretch of steeply sloping vineyards produces the finest and most elegant wines of the Rhineland—full and balanced and long-lived. *Kabinett* wines may last five years and longer, while *Spätlesen* and the various *Auslesen* may last a decade and more.

Hochheim, the easternmost town of the Rheingau, is noted for superior wines. The English of the past century, not caring for the complex German classifications, decided to call all the wines of the region "hocks," and the name has come to stand for all Rhineland white wines, in much the way "claret" stands for all Bordeaux reds.

This worked well in Britain, where distinctions were made solely by price. But that was in the days when wine was plentiful, demand was small and prices low. Today the best wines are scarce and much more individual than they used to be, so the names of the towns are needed. The wines get fuller as you travel west to Rüdesheim. It is surprising how quickly one can learn to identify the wines from the different towns, a learning process so pleasant that some people manage to extend it over a lifetime:

Hochheim	Hattenheim
Eltville	Hallgarten
Rauenthal	Winkel
Erbach	Johannisberg
Kiedrich	Geisenheim
Rüdesheim	

MOSEL-SAAR-RUWER

The lightest wines of the Rhineland come from the Mosel, the tributary that tumbles into the Rhine near Coblenz. Its best section is in a winding stretch just above the city of Trier, where vineyards too steep for tractors, or even for horses or mules, are terraced into the south-facing slopes. Wines lighter still come from vineyards along two smaller streams that empty into the Mosel, the Saar and the Ruwer, but the whole area is considered as a single region. The river rises far south, in France, running along the border of Luxembourg, which also boasts a few white-wine vineyards. Moselle, the French spelling, derives from the ancient Roman, Mosella, but wine lovers are apt to follow the German *der Mosel,* "MO zul."

Whichever way you say it, the wines are among the pleasantest and floweriest in the world, never as heavy

as the sonorous names of the towns they come from. The most famous is Bernkastel, often spelled with a c in the middle.

Wines blended from lesser vineyards are bottled as regionals, principally *Moselblümchen,* quality depending on the excellence of the shippers. There are two other regionals, well-known because of their distinctive labels: *Zeller Schwarze Katz* shows a black cat, *Krover Nacktarsch* shows a boy being spanked.

MOSEL	Piesport
	Bernkastel
	Graach
	Wehlen
	Zeltingen

SAAR	Wiltingen
	Kanzem
	Neidermennig
	Ockfen
	Saarburg

RUWER	Eitelsbach
	Herrenberg
	Käsel

SWEET WHITE WINES

If you were asked to single out the best of all desserts, chances are it would be some incredibly rich cake or pastry. Listening to the discussion, a wine lover might suggest that all such confections were perfectly fine, but nothing can match a ripe pear and a glass of sweet white wine. People would look at him as if he'd lost his mind.

Sweet white wines have been out of fashion for the past couple of generations and it's hard to figure out why. It can't be a matter of calories, because a glass of wine might contain perhaps a hundred, while a piece of cake might add up to three times as much. It can't be scarcity, because every shop offers choices from the famous districts. It can't be price, because the great sweet white wines are the best values available today. Maybe it's just that dry wines have commanded all the attention.

Dry white wines are the ones associated with meals and sweet whites simply don't come to mind when dinner is planned. Mostly, though, people think they are supposed to like dry wines and know about them, so they say they do, and are not supposed to like sweet wines, so they say they don't. The wines really preferred are soft southern wines or flowery northern wines without the sharpness and astringency that come from fruit acids. They do not contrast so strikingly with the often-sweetish savor of our most popular dishes. Chicken, crab, lobster, and dishes like duck prepared with sweet sauces all taste best with wines that aren't too dry. This is all quite confusing to the wine trade, which says that people talk dry but drink sweet, and sees to it that low-priced wines meant for the widest possible market are safely on the sweet side.

Young people usually start out liking wines lightly sweetened because of their similarity to fruit juices and soda pop. Young adults connect sweetness with childish tastes, perhaps buying dry wines because they have decided it's a grown-up thing to do. Older people tend to lose their taste for dryness, gravitating to sweeter and sweeter wines. Admitting to a liking for sweet wines, then, seems to be a sign of immaturity or of old age creeping up. It's too bad that the aura of the wine, not its actual taste, becomes the criterion for judgment.

People have different ideas about what a sweet wine is. Many get confused because everybody uses wine terms so loosely. The range of taste is so wide, the best thing to do is to set up some sort of scale, like the one below:

DRY A wine without sweetness. One that tastes almost puckery, even tart the way an apple is. A wine less sweet than whatever you happen to be eating it with.

SOFT A wine without tartness, with little taste of fruit acids. Something like a blade of grass you might bite into. The taste comes from the glycerine in the grape and from the alcohol. One might call it a wine without dryness.

FLOWERY   A wine that smells and tastes of blossoms, and may even taste of the smell of flowers.

FRUITY   Quite literally, the sweetness of ripe fruit, reminiscent of strawberries or cherries or peaches, but not so pronounced as these.

SWEET   A sweetness like that of syrup or of a custard. There is a wide range. Some taste like the thickest of maple syrups, others like the thinnest of apple ciders.

The thing to do is to taste some sweet wines, not once but several times, so you grow accustomed to what can be expected. The cautious experimenter chills the wine so that it is very cold; coldness masks the sweetness. As the wine warms up in the glass, the sweetness comes out, and you can find the moment when you like it best.

The outstanding characteristic of the best sweet white wines is that they are not cloying, however rich

Up on the Loire, the Chenin Blanc is used to produce the sweet whites of Vouvray and Saumur. The grape of Sauternes, the Sauvignon, makes the dry wines of Pouilly-Fumé and Sancerre. Sauternes outshines them all, so much so that other regions have borrowed the name, usually without the final s; wines so called are pathetic imitations.

and sweet they may be. You may choose to drink only a small glass or two of them, much less than you would drink of a dry wine, simply because one's sweet tooth is quickly satisfied.

The sweet wines to try first are those from the twin Bordeaux districts of Sauternes and Barsac, or the *Auslesen* from the Rhineland. No wines are made more carefully or with more loving attention.

Sauternes is made to be sweet. The vineyards lie south of the Graves district, planted in Sauvignon and Sémillon grapes that are allowed to ripen fully on the vine, then allowed to ripen still more. The grapes are attacked by a mold, *Botrytis cinerea*, called *pourriture noble*, the "noble rot," in France and *Edelfäule* on the Rhine. The resulting concentration of juice makes for a rich wine high in alcohol that can live for a decade and longer. Pickers pass through the vineyards several times during the vintage, picking only bunches that show a lot of mold on the grape skins.

In Germany, the presence of the mold marks the distinction between the *Auslesen* and those *Spätlesen* that are made simply from over-ripe grapes. Most people are satisfied with *Auslesen*, leaving the sweeter grades to those who have cultivated a special taste.

In France, the different grape varieties and climate produce wines quite sweet enough. The undisputed *Grand Cru* is Château d'Yquem, but there are a host of Classed Growths, *Crus Classés*, and lesser vineyards to choose from. Many are bottled by the owners and sold as château-bottlings, but much is sold to the shipper for blending. They are sold as Sauternes or Haut Sauternes, the word "Haut" supposedly identifying the best section of that district. Haut Sauternes might be thought to be sweeter, but hardly anyone can notice differences.

Other sweet wines come from across the river in

Entre-Deux-Mers, from sub-districts of Sainte Croix-du-Mont, Côtes de Bordeaux (the best wine comes from the town of Cadillac), and the half-sweet wines of Sainte-Foy-Bordeaux. The wines are scarcely interesting when true Sauternes is available so inexpensively, and many of the vineyards have turned to producing dry and flowery wines.

There's another way sweet wines are made all around the Mediterranean, and that is to leave the grapes on straw mats to dry in the sun. These wines are called *vins de paille* in France, and *passito* in Italy. Practically every Italian district makes half-sweet or sweet wines from dried grapes, and those called Caluso or Enfer can occasionally be found. After an Italian dinner, a chilled glass of such wine with a bowl of fruit seems to be a perfect ending.

One of the most famous sweet wines is the Tokay of Hungary, made from *Furmint* grapes. Baskets of grapes are hung up and the juice is allowed to ooze out, after which it is fermented. This concentrated

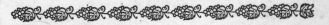

It is also possible to preserve sweetness in the wine by stopping fermentation before it is complete, so that some of the natural sugar remains. Many wines from secondary grapes are so fermented, the sweetness hiding flaws. Originally, various grapes were planted together in the vineyard, the sharp acid of one balancing, say, the excess sugar in another. This is still done wherever sweet wines are made. Both practices are quite sound and practical, providing pleasant wines rather than ones that are unbalanced and odd in taste.

elixir is added to normally fermented wine, the amount added being measured by the amount of wine from the baskets, called *puttonyos*. This grade is called *Aszu*, and the number of *puttonyos* added is noted on the label, 3 or 4 or 5. A still sweeter wine, *Eszencia*, is made from raisinized grapes. One equivalent to a *Spätlese* is called *Szamorodni* and it may be almost dry. Tokay is one of the rarest wines in the world and one of the most expensive; it can last for decades.

With prices of Sauternes so low, however, it is practical to try these first. *Auslesen* from the Rhine deserve exploration, so do the Vouvrays and Saumurs, and *passitos* of Italy. All of them will surprise you with their excellence—wines not to be missed, until everybody discovers how good they are, causing the prices to go up. For the rest of the decade, however, sweet wines will be the bargains of the world of wines.

RED WINES

Red wine is made all around the Mediterranean, most of it consumed in the country of origin. Only a few of the better wines are exported, mostly from France and Italy, Spain and Portugal. Others come from Hungary and Yugoslavia, from the Near East and Africa, and sooner or later there will be wines from Russia.

The good wines are shipped under regional and district names, like Chianti from Italy or Rioja from Spain, although many now come in bearing a name of the grape, like Nebbiolo from Italy or Pinot Noir from Burgundy.

There are hundreds of reds to choose from and the pleasure of wine is to taste the differences. Names become quickly familiar, and some of the least known may please you most.

Generally, the more precise the name, the better the wine. A district wine will be better than one bearing a regional name. A town within the district will offer a better wine than one with the broader denomination. Wines with vineyard names are best of all.

FRANCE

French red wines have delighted the world for half a millennium, their reputation rising with each generation. Two regions stand out, Burgundy and Bordeaux, although superb red wines also come from the Rhone, some good ones from the Loire. There are country wines everywhere, some of them extraordinary. But what most of the French drink most of the time is the wine of the Midi from the south of France, varying only by the degree of alcohol contained: 12% costs more than 11%. For something a little better, the Frenchman will order a regional wine like Bordeaux Supérieur or Beaujolais. Only occasionally will he order something better.

Perhaps all it takes is a sunny day, or the urge to rise above a cloudy one. There may be something new on the menu of his favorite bistro, or the first strawberries may be coming to market, or the first oysters after a hot summer. Whatever the excuse, the French have a tendency to splurge, and the first thing to splurge on is usually wine. A town wine of the Médoc like a Saint Julien, perhaps, or a Beaujolais-Villages. With encouragement, the leap may be all the way to one of the *petits châteaux* of Bordeaux or to a Beaujolais Brouilly or Chiroubles.

If it's spring or the first fine day of autumn, he may try one of the Classed Growths of Bordeaux or even something from Burgundy's Côte d'Or, such as a Monthélie or Santenay. Only on anniversaries or birthdays will he go so far as to try a *Premier Cru* or a *Grand Cru*.

The greatest wines are the easiest to buy. The best Burgundies are marketed as *Grand Cru* or *Premier Cru*. The same words are used for Bordeaux, a few of the best are ranked as *Grand Premier Cru* or *Premier Grand*

Cru, some sixty top vineyards are marketed as *Cru Classé*. These classifications appear on the label. They are all you need to know.

You don't even have to know the name of the wine, the district, the town or the vineyard. Why, then, all the fuss? Because they are all expensive, most of them well over five dollars a bottle, put on the market when they are perhaps four years old, and not yet ready to drink.

The truth is that all the great reds need still more aging, six to ten years for great Burgundy, ten to twenty years for Bordeaux, and sometimes more. Most people don't want to wait that long.

And most people don't want to pay the price. A decade after the vintage, a great red Burgundy can

The French produce nearly two billion gallons of wine a year and drink over 25 gallons per capita, most of it ordinary wine, *vin de table, vin de carafe*. Wine is part of every day, like bread and cheese. Wines from great vineyards are luxuries, like fresh caviar or pheasant, to be drunk by millionaires or film stars. The biggest chain of wine shops in Paris offers such wines for sale only when they are ten years old, and then only as *vins de garde*, wines to lay away in the cellar to be kept years longer before drinking. The sixty or so top Bordeaux vineyards and the thirty or so top Burgundies produce perhaps a million cases of wine in a good year, more than half of which goes abroad—leaving perhaps one bottle a year for one Frenchman out of ten.

cost ten dollars a bottle, a Bordeaux twice that and even more. Such mature reds can cost a hundred dollars a bottle in restaurants. No wonder the French call them wines for special occasions.

Most people can't believe it. Wait until the eighties to drink the 1970 vintage? Who can look that far ahead? They will taste the wine when it comes on the market—some time in 1974—dislike the strong and bitter taste and say they can't see what all the fuss is about. The wine's not ready, of course. They'd have to pay the current price for a 1962 or 1964 to get an idea of what a great wine can be. Fully mature earlier vintages are long gone from the shops, and drinking the rare bottle that does turn up is like drinking diamonds.

And that's why you keep wines.

Even so, there's still an easy way to find wines at modest prices that are ready to drink within four years of the vintage—wines that will taste better than great ones not yet ready.

The better French wines are labeled *Appellation*

Contrôlée. More than 200 place names are protected under the laws, which set standards of production and maximum yield for each one. Some 600,000 of France's more than three million vineyard acres, nearly a thousand square miles, come under these control laws.

Wines somewhat less grand bear a stamp with the initials V.D.Q.S., standing for *Vins Délimités de Qualité Supérieure.* There are some sixty V.D.Q.S. areas, from Provence to the Pyrenees, in the Alps and around the famous districts.

Genuineness is one thing, good wine another, and for that you must depend on the grower or shipper and his importer. A reputable importer's name on the bottle can be more important than anything else. The greater the region, the more the wines can vary from vineyard to vineyard, from vintage to vintage. The only thing to do is to try the wines.

The control laws were necessary to allow wines to compete in foreign markets. This setting of standards protects the buyer, although the larger-than-national market now presents many more wines, and names, to become familiar with. One happy fact is that small growers must band with others to market economically, or join local cooperatives to get the benefits of modern wine technology and the use of expensive equipment like tractors and wine presses and controlled-temperature fermenting tanks and bottling machines. The technology of the past generation has revolutionized the making of good wines as well as great ones, making many more available.

Control laws like those of the French govern all the wines of the European Economic Community, while custom and tradition, often less stringent, govern those of countries not yet members of the E.E.C. In the main regions the Italians, for example, have organizations that supervise the wines, those approved being allowed to show an identifying seal.

For those who want to go beyond the simplest designations, the following lists, country by country and region by region, comprise a buying guide of hundreds of wines. The accompanying comments give some idea of the relative excellence of the various wines. Producers and shippers to look for are Comte de Vogüé, whose vineyard holdings date from 1450, through 17 generations; J. Faiveley; Joseph Drouhin; and Bichot.

BURGUNDY   The heart of Burgundy, where all the great reds come from, is a single slope scarcely thirty miles long, broken in the middle by a quarry. The northern half is the Côte de Nuits, whose only equal is the Haut Médoc of Bordeaux. The least of its wines, usually excellent and often blended, is Hautes-Côtes-de-Nuits, from towns back in the hills. Wines from minor towns and vineyards along the slope are marketed as Côtes-de-Nuits-Villages. Similar categories exist for the southern half, the Côte de Beaune. Together, these two slopes make up the Côte d'Or (Slope of Gold), because the great wines are considered to be liquid gold.

Much of the wine goes to market under the name of the town. When the town boasts a vineyard that is officially rated as a *Grand Cru*, the name of the great growth is tacked to that of the town. This makes it possible for all the wines of the commune to bear the famous name, even though the other wines may scarcely approach its excellence. When produced by good growers or shippers, these town wines can be good, even excellent.

The wines most people like to buy when they can afford them are the *Premiers Crus*, vineyards rated as first growths, just below the *Grands Crus*. In some cases, the first growths equal those with the higher rating, and those from the Côte de Nuits are some of the most prized. The phrase alone identifies a superior wine, although it is customary to put the vineyard name on the label. In both parts of the Côte d'Or, a vineyard ranked as *Grand Cru* is outstanding. The phrase is used elsewhere without official sanction, however. A wine from the Rhone or the Loire so denominated is not in the same class as those from the Golden Slope.

The Burgundy vineyards have been so divided again and again over the years that many of them have several owners, each of whom may make only a few bottles from his plot. Consequently, a single vineyard's wines may vary widely, depending on the vintner's skill, his tending of the vines, the time of harvesting. Some owners bottle their own wines, a practice called estate-bottling, while others sell to shippers, who may choose to blend the wines with other lots from the same vineyard. A buyer must depend on the reputation and skill in tasting of the importer, who must choose the best from a range of wines.

South of the Côte d'Or are the districts of Chalon and Macon, the Côtes Chalonnaise and Maconnaise, where much good, reasonably-priced wine is produced. The pride of Southern Burgundy, however, is the Beaujolais district, famous for wines meant to be drunk young. Those known as Beaujolais-Villages are ranked higher than those called Beaujolais Supérieur or Beaujolais—the best bearing the names of the township, on their labels, where they are produced.

A list of the lesser names can be helpful. They are listed below in ascending order. Not much of the wine simply called Bourgogne Rouge (sold under brand names in France) is exported. The next higher red wine category is called *Passe-tout-grains* in France, a blend of the Pinot Noir, which produces all the great Burgundies, and Gamay, from which Beaujolais is made. Some of these blends can be quite good; they are beginning to appear in the United States under the name Pinot Noir Gamay. Some importers are also marketing blends of Pinot Noir from Southern Burgundy under the grape name:

> Bourgogne Rouge
> Pinot Noir Gamay
> Pinot Noir
> Macon
> Macon Supérieur
> Macon *plus a village name*
> Hautes-Côtes-de-Beaune
> Côtes-de-Beaune Villages
> Hautes-Côtes-de-Nuits
> Côtes-de-Nuits Villages

The reds of the Côte Chalonnaise go to market under township names:

> Mercurey
> Givry

So does the best Beaujolais. Both Mercurey and Givry are fruity, fresh wines made from the Pinot Noir. Beaujolais is made from the Gamay, a much fruitier wine meant to be drunk young within two years of vintage.

Youngest of all is *Beaujolais Primeur*, the new Beaujolais that's rushed to Paris by the middle of November. It's also called *Beaujolais Nouveau* and the grapes picked as early as possible, the juice fermented as quickly as possible, so that Parisians can taste the new vintage. In October, some white grape juice that's still fermenting comes up from Blaye in Bordeaux, and when the signs go up saying Blayais has arrived, everybody has a glass or two. But *Beaujolais Primeur* is the first real wine. Its arrival in Paris trumpets the vintage, and everybody talks about it. Some of it, often sent by air, arrives in New York in time for Christmas.

That's one Beaujolais. There are two others. One is *Beaujolais de l'année*. Beaujolais of the year is meant to be drunk up before the next vintage, arriving in Paris just before spring. Grapes are picked at the normal time, fermented in the usual way, which may take a week or ten days, then drawn off into vats or casks. The short time in wood rounds out the wine, giving it some body. Still fresh and extremely fruity, the wine is a joy to drink. Beaujolais of the year is the darling of the latest generation of French chefs who believe that food should not be elaborate but be made from the best raw materials and be cooked as simply as possible. Beaujolais of the year is the perfect companion.

Dishes of some subtlety—those with a combination of tastes or a perfect but unthickened sauce—call for wines of distinction, however fresh and fruity, and these are Beaujolais from the villages. The wine may require as much as a year in cask. It will improve very little in bottle, although some people feel that wines from areas like Moulin-à-Vent or Morgon reach their prime when three years old. Most of the wines bearing township names are at their best when under two years old. The names of the areas appear on the labels and are listed more or less in order from lightest to fullest:

Fleurie
Chiroubles
Juliénas
Saint Amour
Chénas
Brouilly
Côte-de-Brouilly
Moulin-à-Vent
Morgon

CHATEAU de BUFFAVENT
Beaujolais Supérieur
APPELLATION BEAUJOLAIS SUPÉRIEUR CONTROLÉE
SHIPPED BY: A. BICHOT & Cⁱᵉ, NÉGOCIANTS A BEAUNE, COTE-D'OR, FRANCE
IMPORTED BY SCHENLEY IMPORT Co, NEW YORK, N. Y. - Sole Agents in U.S.A.
Red Burgundy Table Wine   Alcohol 12,5% by Volume   Contents: 1 Pint 8 Fl. Oz.
Produce of France

Wines from neighboring towns are marketed as Beaujolais-Villages. To the south are vineyards producing wines marketed as Beaujolais Supérieur, often good, and Beaujolais, sometimes good. Beaujolais may cost less than two dollars a bottle, while a Moulin-à-Vent can cost as much as four dollars.

Sometimes a meal can call for a rounded wine that

has shown some development in the bottle, one that is perhaps three or four years old, having spent at least a year in wood. Such wines are the lighter Burgundies from the Côte de Beaune, from such communes as:

Savigny
Santenay
Monthélie
Pernand-Vergelesses
Auxey-Duresses
Saint Aubin
Ladoix

The best wines bear the words *Premier Cru* and even the name of the vineyard, with a minimum of 11% alcohol. Wines simply bearing the name of the town have a degree less.

The same pattern holds for the fuller and more famous wines from the major townships of the Côte d'Or. Generally, the great wines from the Côte de Beaune are lighter than those from the Côte de

Wines from these areas are limited in yield per acre and must have by law at least 11% of alcohol. Those marketed as Beaujolais-Villages and Beaujolais Supérieur may have a degree less alcohol, and larger yields are permitted in vineyards from which they come. Beaujolais need have only 9.5%, and still larger yields are permitted. This pattern is followed for all wines coming under *Appellations Contrôlées*.

Nuits. The towns below are listed from south to north, the wines getting generally grander from town to town. Wines of the Beaune slope may take six years to develop, fading after a decade, while those from the Côte de Nuits may require a couple more years and will last perhaps twice as long.

COTE DE BEAUNE	Chassagne-Montrachet
	Puligny-Montrachet
	Meursault*
	Volnay
	Pommard
	Beaune
	Aloxe-Corton

---

* Meursault produces mostly white wines, its reds being marketed as Volnay-Santenots. Reds from a neighboring hamlet are sold as Meursault-Blagny.

COTE DE NUITS   Nuits-Saint-Georges
                 Vosne-Romanée
                 Vougeot
                 Chambolle-Musigny
                 Morey-Saint-Denis
                 Gevrey-Chambertin
                 Fixin

Vineyards in the Côte de Nuits entitled to be called
Grand Cru are produced on scarcely more than 1000
acres. There are something like 5000 acres more,
including First Growths and those entitled only to
town names. The Côte de Beaune is twice as large,
but Corton is the only red wine vineyard entitled to
be called a Great Growth.

The Great Growths do not by law have to bear the
town name. Although they are very expensive, here

for the record, is a list of them. They are comparable
to the eight outstanding vineyards of Bordeaux.

Chambertin and
    Chambertin-Clos-de-Bèze*
Clos-de-Tart
Clos-de-la-Roche
Bonnes-Mares
Clos-Saint-Denis
Musigny
Clos-de-Vougeot
Romanée-Conti
Richebourg
La Romanée
La Tâche
Romanée-Saint-Vivant
Grands-Echézeaux
Echézeaux
Corton

---

* Six other vineyards, in addition to these two, are rated as
Grand Cru and allowed to add Chambertin to their own name:
Charmes or Mazoyères (also adjoining), Griotte, Latricières,
Chapelle and Ruchottes.

First Growths of the Côte de Nuits surpass in quality those of the Côte de Beaune. What's more, many of them should be ranked with the Great Growths, and should be singled out, if only because you might won-

Wines bearing town names are blends from lesser vineyards. Vineyards whose names are known command higher prices, particularly those rated as *Premier Cru*. Because the vineyards are divided, a grower owning various parcels may choose to blend them and sell this as *Premier Cru;* a shipper may do the same with wines he has bought.
A grower bottling a wine from a particular vineyard will put its name and rank on the label, with the phrase *Mise du Domaine*, or a variant, to indicate the wine is an estate-bottling. These are expensive wines, those entitled to be called *Grand Cru* easily commanding ten dollars a bottle after three years or so in cask.

der why some are so expensive. In the old days, the top vineyard in each town was dubbed *Tête de Cuvée*, the "chief vat," and knowing their names may help you in selecting one of two wines from a particular town. An estate-bottled wine is usually prized over those of shippers.

LEADING FIRST GROWTHS

COTE DE NUITS

Fixin	Clos du Chapitre
	Clos de la Perrière
	Clos Napoleon
	Les Hervelets
	Les Arvelets
Gevrey-Chambertin	Clos Saint Jacques
	Varoilles
	Cazetiers
Morey-Saint-Denis	Clos des Lambrays
Chambolle-Musigny	Les Amoureuses
	Les Baudes
Vosne-Romanée	Aux Malconsorts
	Les Beaux-Monts
	Les Suchots
	La Grande Rue
	Les Gaudichots
Nuits-Saint-Georges	Les Saint Georges
	Les Vaucrains
	Les Cailles
	Les Porets
	Les Pruliers
	Clos de la Maréchale
	Clos des Corvées

COTE DE BEAUNE

Aloxe-Corton	Corton Clos-du-Roi
	Corton Bressandes
	Corton Renardes
	Perrières
	Maréchaude
Pernand-Vergelesses	Ile des Vergelesses
Beaune*	Grèves
	Fèves
	Bressandes
	Marconnets
	Clos des Mouches
	Les Teurons
	Les Cras
Pommard	Les Epenots
	Les Rugiens-Bas
Volnay	Les Caillerets
	Champans
	Les Fremiets
	Santenots
Auxey-Duresses	Les Duresses
Monthélie	Les Champs Fulliots
Santenay	Gravières
Chassagne-Montrachet	
	La Boudriotte
	Clos Saint Jean
	Morgeot
	La Maltroie

* For the past few centuries vineyards have been donated to the local hospital in Beaune, the Hospices de Beaune. The wines are sold at auction on the second Sunday of November each year. The wines come from some of the best vineyards along the slope, commanding high prices. The name of the donor is used to identify the wine. Cuvée Charlotte Dumay and Cuvée Docteur Peste, both Cortons, usually command the highest prices. All the wines are generally excellent and help to set prices for the current vintage throughout the Côte d'Or.

BORDEAUX   The largest of the great regions. Much of its red wine is marketed simply as Bordeaux or Bordeaux Supérieur, under the names of the shipper, as brand names or even with vineyard names. Often good buys, the wines are usually ready to drink when put on the market, two or three years after the vintage, but many taste better after another year. Those with vineyard names are called Château so-and-so, a custom that began when most of the good wines came

from large estates dominated by a villa or country house. Ranked above them are several hundred vineyards known as *Cru Bourgeois, Cru Bourgeois Supérieur* and *Cru Exceptionel.*

These phrases appear on the label and many of them are excellent buys, often improving with three or four years in bottle. Altogether, they are known as *petits châteaux*, and it is fashionable now to buy such vineyards and set about improving the quality of the wines by replanting. Reasonable in price, every wine lover has two or three he has discovered, serving them to surprise dinner guests with their excellence.

The most popular wines of Bordeaux, however, are those marketed under the famous district names of Haut Médoc, Graves, Saint Emilion and Pomerol. Best known are those of the Haut Médoc, so numerous that wines are sold under the names of the township. Least known are those of the Médoc to the north, ranked just below Haut Medoc:

Bordeaux	Haut Médoc
Bordeaux Supérieur	Graves
Médoc	Saint Emilion
Pomerol	

BICHOT

MARGAUX

APPELLATION CONTROLÉE

red bordeaux table wine
produce of france
contents 1 pint 8 fl. oz.
alc. 11°5 by volume

IMPORTED BY
SCHENLEY IMPORT Co.
NEW YORK, N. Y.
Sole Agents in U. S. A.
shipped by

ALBERT BICHOT & Cⁱᵉ
NÉGOCIANT-ÉLEVEUR A BORDEAUX GIRONDE

(The towns of the Haut Médoc, going north from Bordeaux, are Margaux, Saint Julien, Pauillac and Saint

Estèphe; generally, the wines get fuller as you go north.)

Sub-districts around Saint Emilion, whose wines are less distinguished, but good buys when sold under the names of the châteaux, are:

> Saint Georges–St. Emilion
> Montagne–St. Emilion
> Lussac–St. Emilion
> Puisseguin–St. Emilion
> Parsac–St. Emilion
> Sables–St. Emilion

Almost unknown districts near Pomerol, which produce some very good wines sold as *petits châteaux,* include:

> Lalande-de-Pomerol
> Côtes-Canon-Fronsac
> Côtes de Fronsac
> Côtes de Bourg
> Premières Côtes de Blaye

The first two, particularly, produce some excellent, full-bodied wines at reasonable prices, practically secret wines known only in France. A few are now being exported and are worth seeking.

All the vineyards are planted in the same grapes but in varying proportion. The Cabernet Sauvignon is the most prized and dominant in the Haut Médoc and Graves, followed by Merlot and Cabernet Franc, dominant in Saint Emilion, Pomerol and its neighbors. Varying proportions influence the character of the wines, the Cabernet Sauvignon producing wine of great distinction but slow to mature, the Merlot contributing richness and softness, Cabernet Franc providing a lightness and the ability to mature readily. Generally, even the lesser vineyards in Haut Médoc and Graves require a decade to mature, while those of Saint Emilion, Pomerol and its neighbors require six years. The best wines spend at least three years in cask before bottling.

The best vineyards of Haut Médoc were rated over a century ago and the classification is still used, although all the other vineyards except Château Haut Brion in Graves were ignored. With modifications and inclusion of vineyards omitted, a listing of the dozen top vineyards in each township can be helpful. With few exceptions, the wines are made and bottled at the vineyards. This practice of château-bottling is a further guarantee of authenticity.

Eight vineyards are universally considered to be outstanding:

> Château Lafite-Rothschild
> Château Margaux
> Château Latour
> Château Haut-Brion
> Château Mouton-Rothschild
> Château Cheval Blanc
> Château Ausone
> Château Pétrus

MARGAUX   Wines noted for lightness and elegance. The town nearest to Bordeaux, Margaux is also used for vineyards in neighboring Cantenac and other communes. All the vineyards seek to approach the rich bouquet and balance of qualities of its greatest wine, Château Margaux, from which the town gets its name.

Rausan-Ségla
Rauzan-Gassies
Brane-Cantenac
Durfort-Vivens
Palmer
Lascombes
Cantenac-Brown
Giscours
d'Issan
Malescot-Saint-Exupéry
Prieuré-Lichine
Kirwan

SAINT JULIEN   Considered to be the most typical of the district's wines, somewhat fuller than those of Margaux.

Léoville-Las-Cases
Léoville-Poyferré
Léoville-Barton
Ducru-Beaucaillou
Gruaud-Larose
Beychevelle
Branaire-Ducru
Talbot
Gloria
Langoa-Barton
Saint-Pierre
Lagrange

PAUILLAC   In addition to three of the greatest clarets—Lafite, Latour and Mouton—the township boasts a particularly distinguished group of full-bodied

wines that are exceptionally long-lived, some still at
their peaks after twenty years.

> Pichon-Longueville
> Pichon-Longueville-Lalande
> Lynch-Bages
> Duhart-Milon
> Mouton-Baron-Philippe
> Grand-Puy-Lacoste
> Grand-Puy-Ducasse
> Pontet-Canet
> Batailley
> Haut-Batailley
> Croizet-Bages
> Haut-Bages-Libéral

SAINT ESTEPHE & OTHERS   Regionals from
the town, together with those from Saint Julien, are
the most popular of the Médoc. The wines are fuller
than most of the others. There are fewer outstanding
vineyards, but many bourgeois growths. Others from
various hamlets that deserve attention are included
here, for convenience.

> Calon-Ségur
> Cos d'Estournel
> Montrose
> Cos Labory
> Capbern
>
> La Lagune
> Cantemerle
> Chasse-Spleen
> Dutruch-Lambert
> Gressier-Grand-Poujeaux
> La Tour-de-Mons

GRAVES   In addition to Haut Brion, Graves boasts of many other fine châteaux and a good many minor ones. The following list is limited to those officially rated as *Crus Classés*, although people are continually finding others that they like at reasonable prices, often below three dollars a bottle.

> La Mission-Haut-Brion
> Haut-Bailly
> * Domaine de Chevalier
> Fieuzal
> * Carbonnieux
> * Malartic-Lagravière
> * Latour-Martillac
> Latour-Haut-Brion
> Smith-Haut-Lafitte
> * Olivier
> * Bouscaut
> Pape-Clément

NOTE: Those marked with asterisks produce fine white wines, as well as reds. Château Couhins and Laville-Haut-Brion produce only whites.

SAINT EMILION   The wines of Saint Emilion were officially classified in the fifties, but not very helpfully for the consumer. A dozen were rated First Great Growths but more than sixty others were rated as Great Growths, nobody admitting to anything less. The wines are fuller but less distinguished than those of Haut Médoc and Graves, their bigness causing them to be dubbed "the Burgundies of Bordeaux," which lessens the confusion for some. People like them because they are ready to drink in six years or so and because there are lots of good vineyards competing with each other, thus helping to keep the price down. We list the *Premiers Grands Crus Classés* here, but wines rated as *Grands Crus Classé* are worth hunting.

Cheval Blanc
Ausone
Beauséjour-Duffau
Beauséjour-Fagouet
Belair
Canon
Clos Fourtet
Figeac
La Gaffeliére-Naudes
Magdelaine
Pavie
Trottevieille

POMEROL   The wines of this smallest of the great districts are not yet classified and many vie for first place, right after Château Pétrus. The wines are considered lighter than Saint Emilions, but they are rich and full, nonetheless. The dozen listed are among the largest producers.

Beauregard
Clinet
l'Evangile
Gazin
La Conseillante
Lafleur-Pétrus
La Pointe
Latour-Pomerol
Nenin
Petit-Village
Trotanoy
Vieux-Château-Certan

RHONE   After Burgundy and Bordeaux, the Rhone is a relief—only a few wines sold by district names. Châteauneuf-du-Pape, Hermitage and Côte Rôtie, plus the regional bottled as Côtes-du-Rhone, are the only reds generally available. Ten million gallons of Côtes-du-Rhone are made in a good year, soft and drinkable wines just right for everyday. The popularity of Beaujolais has led to fast vinification and prompt bottling of some Côtes-du-Rhone, shipped to Paris before Christmas, where they are received with some enthusiasm, because of their price, and more skepticism from those who think there's nothing like Beaujolais.

Vineyards are scattered from Lyon to Avignon, a score of grape varieties are used, and while a few town and vineyard names are identified on labels, most of the wines are blends and the district names are enough to ensure finding satisfactory bottles. Because the region is south, vintages are less important than in other districts, the weather more likely to affect quantity than quality. A leading shipper is Delas Frères.

Generally, the wines are big, which means robust and full, which is to say that they are high in alcohol with plenty of taste—just the thing for hearty dishes. Several splendid white wines are made, but in small quantities. The large district of Tavel produces the best rosé of France, but the reds are the ones to seek out, generally superior to all others from the Mediterranean basin.

CHATEAUNEUF-DU-PAPE

When Avignon was the papal seat in the Middle Ages, a summer castle was built for the popes in the midst of old vineyards. The castle is gone but not the vines. They produce one of the world's most popular wines, a million gallons in a good year, but maybe only half that if there's too much rain or too little sun. The wines have the highest minimum of all those coming under *Appellation Contrôlée*, 12½% alcohol, although it is usually at least a degree above that. Oddly enough for such a heady wine, it is ready to drink three years after the vintage, at its best when five years old, fading after ten. The best wines are estate-bottled. Best-known vineyards include Domaine de Mont Redon, Château Fortia, Château de la Nerthe, Château de Vaudieu, but there are many others.

HERMITAGE

A slope a couple of miles long and a couple of hundred yards wide produces the sturdiest wine of France. Its steep vineyards begin fifty miles south of Lyon. In a good year some 40,000 cases of red wine are made, and half as much white. The reds are kept four years in wood, becoming rich and vel-

vety after a couple more years in bottle, and living on
for decades. Even the whites take five years to mature,
Bordering the slope is an area called Crozes-Hermitage,
which produces lesser wines. Almost uniquely among
the great wines of France, Hermitage is blended from
various sections of vineyard and sold under brand
names.

COTE ROTIE   A slope that is steeper and smaller
than that of Hermitage, and only slightly less rugged,
produces Côte Rôtie. Much of the average production
of 12,000 cases is drunk in Lyon, twenty miles away.
The wine stays in cask for five years and needs almost
as much time in bottle before it is ready to drink.
There are two sections, the Côte Brune and the Côte
Blonde, the blond supposedly producing lighter wines.
Most of them are blended, however; the result is a
deeply colored distinctive wine that is rich and full,
with a bouquet that reminds you of truffles and violets,
or even raspberries.

Other wines are similarly likened to fruits and
flowers—and there is no question that Côte Rôtie has
a distinctive aroma.

The bouquet of a wine is generally called the
"nose" by tasters, who shy away from analogies
and prefer to say that Côte Rôtie smells like Côte
Rôtie. This isn't much help, until you try a bottle
for yourself, and then you know at once what the
expert tasters mean. It's big wine with a strong
aroma, and it tastes wonderful.

COTES-DU-RHONE   Pleasant wines, full and rounded and ready to drink a couple of years after the vintage, come from vineyards scattered along the Rhone for more than a hundred miles. They are consistently among the best low-priced wines available. A few village wines stand out, notably Gigondas and Cairanne, names occasionally found on bottles. The separate district of Cornas produces a red that matures well. In most cases, however, a wine labeled simply Côtes-du-Rhone is all you need to look for. It is generally the best wine available in its price class.

ITALY

Italy produces more wine, over two billion gallons, and drinks more, over 40 gallons per capita, than any other country. The claim is made that there are over 1500 different wines, of which 400 are marketed, and some 200 come under D.O.C., *Denominazione di Origine Controllata*. The best reds come from the Piedmont, in the foothills of the Alps, a region that produces more wine than the United States and Russia put together.

Vines grow everywhere in Italy. Most of the wine is made to be drunk in the neighborhood within months of the vintage, so every locality produces a range of wines to meet all needs. Reds or whites may predominate, but various tinges of pink wine can be found, ranging from dry to sweet (Italians are fond of half-sweet wines), and there are various grades at different prices. Cooperatives have sprung up everywhere to handle the wide assortment of grapes, each making a variety of wines. Drinking becomes an adventure.

Word gets around that a particular wine is perfect

at the moment. Everybody drinks that for a few weeks until it's gone, then somebody finds another. Choices change with the season, matched to the foods available in the markets. Brand names of the big firms provide a steady supply of dry reds and whites—in Rome it's Frascati, in Florence it's Chianti—and bulk wines that may come from anywhere. There's always a new wine to try.

Those exported are the northern reds that round out after two or three years in bottle, following a stay in wood for as long as three years. Chianti in straw-covered flasks is one of the few young reds exported; although Bardolino and Valpolicella are best young, those under three years old are hard to find.

The great grape of the Piedmont is the Nebbiolo, where it produces a pair of wines considered Italy's best, Gattinara and Barolo, as well as Barbaresco. The Nebbiolo is also responsible for the wines of Valtellina in neighboring Lombardy, and also Carema, from high up near the French border. Other grapes include Grignolino, Freisa and Barbera, in that order of quality. All across northern Italy are other grapes of local renown, as well as hybrids and those from France and Germany.

The great grape of Chianti is the Sangiovese, grown in the vineyard with some Canaiolo, Trebbiano and Malvasia. All of these are used elsewhere; the grape names identify many of the Italian country wines, like the Lambrusco so popular in Bologna. District names are also common, i.e. the Bardolino and Valpolicella from around Lake Garda.

Dozens of the districts now have symbols on their neck labels, indicating that the wines meet standards set by organizations of local growers. In districts producing the wines mentioned above, the organizations are significant, definitely controlling the quality of wine for export, but elsewhere serving only to identify the wines of the region. Shippers' names you might like to look for on labels are Franco-Fiorina, Negrar, and Verrazzano.

BAROLO The great wine of Italy, full and dark and strong (usually over 13% alcohol), is aged at least three years in wood, a hearty wine for hearty dishes. It improves greatly in the bottle, and the best can last for decades. Authenticity is guaranteed by two district associations, the neck label of one bearing a gold lion, that of the other a centurion's helmeted bust.

BARBARESCO Lighter than Barolo, although made from the same Nebbiolo grape and in much the same way, it rounds out after a couple of years in

bottle and may begin to fade a decade after the vintage. Like its neighbor, it is the wine to serve with rich dishes including white truffles, which are the specialty of nearby Alba. Wines approved by the local growers' association have the gold tower of the township on the neck label.

GATTINARA   Ranked with Barolo, wines of the township are prized because they are rare. Lighter than its peer, the wine still needs three years in bottle to round out after its three years in wood. It is an excellent wine to serve with roasts, like a leg of lamb, or rich stews.

NEBBIOLO   The grape name is used for several wines of the Piedmont, particularly for those from around Alba that border the townships of Barolo and Barbaresco, identifying wines that are generally lighter than those. Even so, a Nebbiolo may continue to develop for as long as a decade, and is full enough to serve with game and wildfowl.

Italians claim only 4% of their wine is exported, although much of what's left is made into brandy and industrial alcohol. Variation in the wine is enormous, depending on the whim of the winemaker or the quality of the grapes. Some small producers make fine wines, snapped up by restaurants and knowing Italians. Most of the wine exported is from large growers and shippers, who have international reputations to maintain.

BARBERA   The grape most widely planted in the Piedmont. Its fullest wines are those from vineyards between Alba and Asti. Frequently left four years in wood, the wines need time in bottle to round out; after a couple of years, they resemble the wines of the Rhone. The best of them are quite dry and robust, although some are made into wines with a sweet overtone.

CAREMA   From vineyards around the town that names it, high in the foothills at nearly 2000 feet. The grapes are trained on pergolas and the overhead trellises form cool and shadowed arbors on a hot day. Perhaps the lightest of the quality wines from the Nebbiolo, it is ready to drink four years after the vintage.

FREISA   A grape that abounds in the Piedmont, the best of its light wines come from Chieri, near Turin; those of Asti are famous. The wines need at least a year in bottle, perhaps more. Freisa di Chieri may be as light as 10% in alcohol, making it a good red wine for summer, served cool.

GRIGNOLINO   A grape that thrives near Asti, its wine is lighter in color than Freisa, and particularly appealing when served young and fairly well chilled. It can be quite high in alcohol, even 13%. The wine generally has an orange tint, but its most distinctive characteristic is a flowery perfume.

VALTELLINA   Most famous wines of Lombardy, the mountainous province lying east of the Piedmont, the Valtellina rank with Barolo and Gattinara. Wines from the terraced vineyards are made from the same grape, Nebbiolo, with an admixture of local varieties. The vineyards stretch along the narrow valley of the Adda River, on the lower slopes of a mountain wall that rises to 12,000 feet and forms the border with Switzerland. The best wines of the district come from vineyards lying east of Sondrio, variously called Sassella, Grumello and Inferno. The deep, darkly crimson wines, full and hard when young, may take a decade to develop. Sassella is the firmest of all, but even the softer Grumello needs at least four years in bottle; Inferno generally has to age at least five years in bottle.

VALPOLICELLA   Grown in vineyards near Lake Garda above Verona, Valpolicella is one of the world's pleasantest carafe wines, but the best grades—from the townships of Negrar, Fumane, Marano, San Pietro Incariano and Sant'Ambrogio—are kept eighteen months in wood. After a year in bottle they are smooth and fruity light wines and remain delightful for another year. It's a short life for a wine that needs such development, but a merry one for the drinker. They are best slightly cool, with practically any light dish.

BARDOLINO   The town and vineyards are on Lake Garda's eastern shore, the exposure and lighter soil accounting for the fact that this wine is slightly lighter than its partner, Valpolicella. It is one of the most charming wines of Italy, rarely over 11% in alcohol, and at its best when less than three years old; Italians sometimes like it older, when it has lost some of its fruitiness.

ROSSO PICENO   Districts that have been successful marketing wines abroad frequently go beyond the regional specialty and offer wines usually available only in Italy. An example is Cupramontana, the town

that produces the best wine of The Marches, Verdicchio. The cooperative there also offers one of the country reds produced in some of the oldest vineyards of Italy, Piceno Rosso. From hills at the southern end of the province close to the Adriatic come the usual variety of wines, the best of which is red, although whites and rosés, various sweet wines and a sparkling wine are also made.

CHIANTI   The enchanting wine of ancient Tuscany comes from a sea of vineyards around Florence, reaching along the valley of the Arno and its tributaries, billowing up into the hills—south to Siena, west to Pisa, north to Pistoia, southeast to Arezzo. The province produces 100 million gallons of wine in a good year, and perhaps half of this ocean is sold as Chianti, marketed cheaply in the straw-covered bottle known

as *fiasco*. The best Chiantis of the region come from districts with ever-tighter controls, where production amounts to about a tenth of the total, the most honored being Chianti Classico.

Classic Chiantis come from a couple of hundred square miles of vineyard south of Florence and extending almost to Siena. Many are produced on large estates of noble families who are active in the local growers' association. The symbol on the neck seal of a Chianti Classico is the *Marco Gallo*, a black cockerel on a gold bull's eye.

A small area of hill vineyards close to Florence produces wines called Chianti Colli Fiorentini.

Plenty of good Chianti comes from outside the

zona classica, like Chianti Montalbano Pistoiese from northwest Florence. Its peer is Chianti Rufina, from northeast of Florence. Another small area produces wines called Chianti dei Empolesi from vineyards on the road to Pisa. Lesser wines come from the other areas: Colli Senesi, Colline Pisane, Colli Aretini, Colline d'Elsa.

Some Chiantis are best when young and these come in the bulging straw-covered *fiaschi*. They have a fizzy, prickly quality in the mouth called *frizzante* in Italy. This comes from tiny bubbles in the wine which result from a slight second fermentation in the bottle. The pleasant sensation is brought about by setting aside as much as ten percent of the grapes on straw mats and letting them dry until they are almost raisins. They are crushed in late November and as their juice begins to ferment it is added to the wine whose fermentation has just ended. This secondary fermentation in the bottle also softens the wine and gives it an undertone of fruitiness. The practice is called *governo* and has proved so successful for Chianti that other regions have begun to follow suit.

Not all Chiantis are made this way, the method being reserved for those meant to be drunk young. Those meant to age are made in the usual way, spending as long as three years in cask before being put into regular bottles. The wines are full and have a big bouquet, the best lasting for a decade or longer. The difference between the two kinds of Chianti is comparable to the difference between a Beaujolais and a Burgundy from, say, the Côte de Beaune. The great houses also produce wines usually called *Riserva*, meant to be kept for longer than a decade. Some of their labels don't even mention the fact that they are Chiantis; their high price makes them easy to identify.

Many firms have begun making white Chianti, and

even rosés, wines to try when you find you like a particular grower's reds. Even the reds, particularly those meant to be drunk young, taste best when cool to the lips, at something like 65°, while the whites and rosés should be cold, below 60°.

LAMBRUSCO   The pet of Bologna, Lambrusco is lightly sparkling and somewhat sweet, producing a froth when poured with gusto—which it usually is. It

is a true *frizzante*, making many more bubbles on the glass than the lightly prickly Chianti, and Italians love it with rich foods, that of Bologna being just about the richest. The wine is becoming popular in America because of its cheerful appearance.

ASTI SPUMANTE   The Italians are fond of wines that sparkle and foam, calling them *spumante*, and these are produced all over Italy. The most popular of all is that from Asti in the Piedmont, made from Moscato grapes. Aromatic and lightly sweet, it is made by fermenting the wine in closed vats, the Charmat process, named after its inventor, which is said to preserve the fragrance of the grape. The traditional method of Champagne, whereby the wine is fermented in bottle, is used by Italian firms to make dry sparkling wines, usually from the Pinot Blanc. Such wines sell for twice the price of Asti Spumante, and both of them are much cheaper than the Champagne of France. The association of producers uses for its neck labels the figure of Asti's patron, San Segundo, a blue figure on a gold background.

PORTUGAL

Portugal drinks most of the table wines it produces, some 25 gallons per capita. Most of it is Vinho Verde from the north, meant to be drunk young. Some of the best wines come from Dão vineyards just south of the Douro Valley, its reds being to the Portuguese what Chianti is to the Italians or Beaujolais to the French.

Sandy seacoast vineyards near Lisbon produce a light red called Colares, not often exported, perhaps because of the growing popularity of the fuller wines of Dão. Modern technology has revolutionized the quality of Portuguese wines, increasing the overseas demand for them.

DAO   A full red wine that is matured more than three years in cask, it has a richness and body like that of a Châteauneuf-du-Pape from the Rhone or a Barolo from the Italian Piedmont. It is a wine to serve with roasts and grilled meats or hearty stews. The Portuguese custom of serving a light and fresh white with a simply cooked fish, then following this with a full Dão with the meat course, contrasting the wines and the dishes, provides a wide range of tastes that makes for lively parties.

SPAIN

The outstanding wine of Spain is the Rioja, planted and extended before the turn of the century by French immigrants. The wines are usually light, the reds being extremely long-lived. When old, they are some of the most astonishing wines to be had, rounded and marvelously velvety. Many of them are kept two or three years in cask and are rarely marketed until they have had at least another year in bottle. Vineyards around Barcelona, particularly Panadès, produce reds that are fuller and ready within a couple of years of the vintage, while others come from Alella and Perelada, which are noted more for whites. South of Madrid is the red wine region of Valdepeñas, generally inexpensive, but remarkably good when well selected. Spanish table wines are increasing in popularity, and one to look for is Siglo, which comes in a unique burlap-covered bottle.

RIOJA   Particularly distinguished are wines made from Bordeaux grapes, the Cabernets and Merlots. The popularity of the wines has permitted the introduction of modern technology, expensive and complex, in recent years, enhancing still more their desirability. Not as well known as those from France and Italy, they are excellent bargains.

ROSÉ WINES

Rosés are cheerful things, like flowers on a table. Red wines can be noble, majestic, full of subtlety, like a soaring symphony. White wines can be lordly, too, gracious and rich and complex, like chamber music. Pink wines are like musical comedy, bright and entertaining, made up of young love and springtime.

Every region makes them, everybody likes them, the way one likes pretty girls or a nice day. They range from pale crimson and light garnet to wines barely tinged with pink or orange, all the way to those that are said to be the pale topaz of a partridge eye, *oeil de perdrix*. Tastes go from tart and dry through flowery to fruity and soft; some of them are even sweet. Many are light in body, meaning almost watery in taste, but many more are full, tasting very much of wine.

People like rosés, because they are supposed to go with anything, without the fuss and folderol so often connected with drinking reds and whites, and producers go along. Although because of their tendency to lightness and mildness of taste, and because they are served chilled, pink wines are most pleasing when drunk in place of white wines. A particular group of them comes from Provence.

The best rosés are made from red wine grapes, the pressed juice being left with the skins only long enough to pick up the desired color. The juice is then drawn off and allowed to finish fermenting by itself. The wines are put in cask for a short time, if at all, then quickly bottled and shipped, to be drunk up within a year or so of the vintage.

Excellent rosés come from the great districts and the noble grapes. Centuries ago, all the red wines of

Bordeaux were light in color and called *clairet*, from which the English adapted their word for red Bordeaux, even when claret came to be a deeply colored wine. Nowadays, Bordeaux rosé is made from Cabernets and even other grapes, generally full and fruity. As full is the rosé of Burgundy made from the Pinot Noir, in the district of Marsannay, just north of the Côte d'Or. The Gamay is used in various regions to make fruity pink wines. All over Italy local grapes are used to make rosés, the same practice being followed in Portugal and Spain.

PORTUGAL

The favorite word to describe rosé is refreshing, some of the most refreshing rosés coming from Portugal. Portuguese rosés have always been popular abroad, if only because one thinks of France and Germany and Italy in terms of red wines and white.

Portugal's reds and whites are also pronounced in taste, so it was sensible of the Portuguese to develop a wine that would be light and soft. Their whites were fine for simple fish dishes, the reds for roasts and hearty stews, but something else was needed with spicy fish dishes and those based on rice brought back from the orient by explorers and the merchantmen that followed after.

When taxes on French wines were raised in England after the loss of the colony of Bordeaux, the wines of

Portugal became popular in London. By the middle of this century, the most popular table wine from Portugal was the rosé called Mateus, a brand name Michel Dreyfus decided to introduce into this country. America was just discovering wines, in the wake of prohibition, depression and war. A wine that would go with anything, making a dinner party festive, was just the thing. Mateus has become the most popular wine imported into the United States, the added market making it the most popular brand in the world. Soft, not tart, it is the wine that's decided on when the choice between red and white is difficult.

TAVEL   As wine drinking became fashionable in the fifties outside international and diplomatic circles, French wines came to be accepted as the ultimate because of the supremacy of Burgundy and Bordeaux. Buying them was not a simple matter, however, because of the complexity of names. Many people solved the problem by inquiring which was the greatest rosé of France. Discovering it was Tavel, they settled on that.

Tavel is near Avignon, a large district planted in a grape good only for rosé, the Grenache. It produces a surprisingly full wine with a big bouquet, usually quite heady because it is generally 13% in alcohol. It is a bright, light crimson with plenty of taste, substantial enough to stand up to a steak or a roast. The district is large, producing something close to half a million gallons a year, much of it coming from a large and modern cooperative. And the wine is reasonable in price. It has become a standard on nearly every wine list in the country, the one to order when Burgundy and Bordeaux are too expensive and choice of other wines is limited. It is at its best well chilled and less than two years old.

Demand for Tavel has grown so great that the wines

of a neighboring district are now being exported. Lirac is also made from the Grenache, but the wine is lighter and less pronounced in taste, an advantage when meals are light. Less well-known, it is therefore much less expensive, which will only increase its popularity. The Grenache is used to produce other rosés along the Rhone; also light and refreshing they are now beginning to be marketed abroad.

ANJOU   The Loire has always been famous for light wines, *the* wines for luncheons and buffets. The white wines are much more distinctive, thanks to modern methods, but the one that still fits the old idea is the rosé from Anjou. Made from local grapes, the wine has a faintly orange cast and a lightly sweet taste, making it particularly suitable for foods like crabmeat or lobster salad, or cold chicken. Pink wines are made all along the Loire, particularly in the Touraine, and some of the leading producers have begun using Cabernets to make fuller and drier pink wines which are now beginning to come on the market.

CHAMPAGNE

Of all the things added to wines, bubbles are the greatest. The night they invented Champagne was as grand for the human animal as the day Noah landed on the Mount and planted a vineyard. Nothing says hooray like Champagne, except fireworks, both of which produce the same response. Champagne has the advantage because you can not only see the excitement but taste it too.

Champagne wasn't invented, of course, but discovered. All of us come upon it in just the way the old monk did—pulling the cork, pouring, looking at the astonishing foam of bubbles, and wondering what it's going to taste like. The monk credited with getting the idea of stuffing a bottle with cork instead of an oiled wad of cloth was the cellarmaster of Hautvillers, and chances are he wasn't at all sure what was going to happen when he pulled the cork out again.

In the last days of the eighteenth century vintners knew that wines kept making bubbles long after the fermentation had ended. They believed it was the drawn-out ending of the tumultuous action and not until this century was it proved that this faint bubbling was the sign of a second fermentation altogether. There was no need to know what it was in order to use it, however. They figured it was the last of the yeast working on the last of the sugar and, in effect, this was so. By adding a little more yeast and sugar they could increase the action. By capturing the bubbles, the wine could be made to sparkle. And that's where the monk's cork went in.

I'm drinking stars, the monk is always quoted as saying, although it was probably less poetic and more exclamatory. What usually happens when you taste a great wine is that you don't say anything at all for a moment, then you burst into a wondering laugh. That's what the monk probably did, clapping his nearest companion on the back with excitement. That's what most people do today, pleased to be tasting anything so good.

The corking and the dosage added to the wine so that a second fermentation would take place in the bottle, were all worked out in the next couple of decades. It took nearly half a century to solve the problem of the bottles, which kept bursting.

There were fireworks in the Champagne cellars all too often during those first years of bottle fermentation. The captured carbonic acid gas that is the by-product of yeast working on sugar to make alcohol could build up a pressure of six atmospheres. Bottles couldn't take the strain, and when one exploded others followed. Sometimes half the bottles blew up with a merry popping, making rivers of foam. The people of Champagne still hate the sound of a cork popping, and the proper way to open a bottle of the bubbly is to make the cork come out with a sigh.

Producing bottles thick enough to withstand pressure and getting just the right dosage so that enough bubbles would result was a matter of trial and error. The safety factor of today's bottles is so great that a bursting bottle is unknown, although it is still customary to wrap a bottle in a towel as it is being opened, just in case.

The first Champagnes were sweet. The French had plenty of dry wines from Bordeaux and Burgundy, not to mention the Rhone and the Loire, so a bubbly sweet wine was just right for afternoon sipping and evening celebration. After Waterloo, the Russians occupied the province east of Paris while the peace treaties were hammered out, and the troops fell in love with Champagne. During the last half of the last century Czarist Russia was Champagne's major customer and the wines couldn't be made sweet enough. The English changed all that.

The English made the modern world of wines. Massee's law states that he who has the market holds the trade, and the British shipped wines to the ends of the empire. The sun always set on an Englishman holding a glass. Sweet wines like Sherry and Port were invented to please the English, claret of Bordeaux and hocks from the Rhine were suited to their taste. With plenty of sweet wines, as well as cakes with tea, Victorian Englishmen decided they wanted Champagne dry.

The obliging French devised the English *Cuvée* to please London, a Champagne with just enough sugar to put bubbles in the wine but not enough to give it a sweet taste. The turn of the century was also a time of sweet cordials and liqueurs, the beginning of the fashion for aperitifs which were bittersweet. And so there was a place for dry Champagne in fashionable Paris. The place was Maxim's.

The English led European aristocracy and the American wealthy to the Champagne suppers at Maxim's, where corks popped loudly and beauties scuffled for gold coins flung by Russian princes, German counts, English lords and American railroad barons. Sweet drinks wouldn't do because they quickly pall, and dry Champagne in the English style suited the laughter and the lobster and the love-making. An evening at Maxim's was the ultimate as Victoria's reign came to a close, and every city tried to create places like it. Dry Champagne became the fashion, the very symbol of carefree luxury. The popping cork was a signal for the revelry to commence.

So that you could select the degree of dryness you preferred, Champagne producers made *Sec*, which was dry; *Extra Sec*, which was very dry; and *Brut*, which was driest of all. English *Cuvée* was mostly *Extra Sec*, a wine that was delicious with caviar or *foie gras* or truffled chicken or anything else that was expensive. *Brut* was drunk with anything that did not have a sweet savor, but it was really best by itself—and a frivolous companion. Champagne producers continued to make sweeter styles for their old markets, but producers in other regions soon took to sparkling their wines in order to grab some of the business. Other wines were not as good for sparkling as Champagne, but their flaws could be hidden under sweetness and could be sold more cheaply. Finally, Champagne producers were hard put to meet the demand for their dry wines.

One of the best sparkling wines comes from Vouvray in the Loire. The still wine is naturally soft and sweet in good vintages, but may be dry and hard in poor ones. These lesser wines are used for sparkling. St. Péray in the Rhone does the same thing, as do some of the producers in the Savoie. The grapes of Champagne are also planted in Burgundy, and Burgundians saw no reason why they couldn't sparkle wines as well as their neighbors to the north. Sparkling Burgundy was never popular until it was decided to make it out of red wines. The red remained unpopular in France, but not so in the United States where it quickly became a favored wine.

With the years, less expensive methods than fermentation in the bottle were devised. The Charmat process consists of fermenting the wine in sealed vats and bottling under pressure. This "Bulk Process" is forbidden in Champagne as are any but the traditional fermentation in bottle, and when the less satisfactory method is used elsewhere, the fact is usually stated on the label. Another method, called the "Star Process," involved collecting the gas from the fermenting wine, then putting it back in the wine. Wines are also simply carbonated, the way bubbles are added to water to make soda. No such wines compare to those made by "La Méthode Champenoise," the wine resting for two or more years after completing its second in-bottle fermentation. After that the bottle is gradually shaken and tipped up on its neck until the sediment settles against the seal in the neck of the bottle. The bottle is then disgorged of the sediment, some of the same wine is used to fill the bottle, and dosed with the sweetening used to produce the various degrees of sweetness. The wine is again stored until ready for shipment. The process takes well over four years and Champagnes are rarely sent to market until they are six years old. They are ready to drink when marketed, and most of them last for a decade longer.

The French call a sparkling wine *vin mousseux*—those wines not dosed but bottled quickly are called *pétillant*—and they drink more of it than anybody else. This is not extravagance, because the French tax on sparkling wine is low. Foreign governments, however, put high taxes on sparkling wines, as much as two or three dollars a bottle, so that it is truly a luxurious wine. Importers continually struggle to get the tax on bubbles reduced, to no effect. Domestic producers, who freely borrow the word "Champagne" to give their sparkling wines an aura of excellence, if not the actuality, join in protesting, but the exorbitant tax continues. It is the same for all sparkling wines; Champagne being so much better than its imitators, by comparison it offers the best value for the money spent.

In exceptional years, vintage Champagnes are made, but even then a portion of the crop is a blending of wines in which the vintage is balanced with another. The blending is called a *cuvée*, or vatting, the process producing excellent wines reasonable in price, considering the extensive attention the wines receive.

Blending becomes malpractice only when good wines are made less good. This is particularly true for types of wines made by adding to the simple ferment

To open Champagne properly, you turn the bottle not the cork. The wire muzzle around the neck is twisted loose by turning a loop in the wire counterclockwise. Then the cork is grasped in one hand while the other hand turns the bottom of the bottle. The hand on the cork covers the cork so that it won't fly off. Turning with the hand that holds the bottom of the bottle provides plenty of leverage because of the generous size of the base. A towel can be wrapped around the bottle if it's slippery, but when the wine is poured its label should be exposed so that people can see what they are going to be drinking.

—bubbles in the case of Champagne, brandy in the case of Sherry and Porto. Even table wines can be balanced, as when a thin wine of one vintage is combined with a heavy wine of another, to produce a non-vintage wine better than what went into it. In a sense, blending takes place in the vineyard, when various grapes are planted together, each having a positive effect on

the finished wine. Blending is bad when wines are "stretched," inferior wines being added to make a superior wine go further. The complex control laws throughout the European Community are expressly designed to prevent this.

Champagne particularly benefits from blending. The main towns of the district are Ay and Epernay, along a stretch of the Marne some eighty miles west of Paris. To the north is the Montagne de Reims. The Pinot Noir is planted in both sections. Running south from the river is the Côte des Blancs, its vineyards planted in Pinot Blanc, which produces a lighter, more delicate wine than does the Pinot Noir. Some of it is bottled alone to produce *Blanc de Blancs*, white wine from white grapes, the most delicate of all Champagnes.

Champagne has long been a full-bodied wine, however, and this is brought about by blending the wine of Pinot Blanc and Pinot Noir together. The black grapes are pressed and fermented away from the skins so that

the juice doesn't pick up any color. In December, when the fermentation has finished, master blenders make up their *cuvées* according to their ideas of what will produce the best Champagne. In general, there are two styles.

Some houses prefer to produce Champagnes that are called *franc et loyal*, full wines in the old tradition of the district. One such firm is Krug. The popularity in recent years of *Blanc de Blancs* has encouraged many such houses to offer that style, but the old tradition is adhered to for the other Champagnes in the line.

Other firms specialize in making light Champagnes,

using more wines from the Côte des Blancs in each *cuvée*. There is not one Champagne, but many, and most people like several different styles.

Most firms also offer pink Champagne, made by leaving juice of the Pinot Noir on the skins for a time to pick up color. These are generally fuller in taste than regular Champagnes with less nuance of taste.

The most popular style of Champagne these days is the one called *Brut*, the driest generally available. It is a perfect wine to drink by itself, but too dry for most foods. It is also the most expensive. Those labeled *Extra Sec*, slightly more fruity in taste, generally taste best with foods. Occasionally found is *Champagne Nature*, made by adding no sugar at all, but the wine is almost parchingly dry, tasting best after dinner.

SPARKLING WINES

Some excellent sparkling wines other than Champagne, but rarely as dry, are made and are worth trying. Perhaps the best come from Saumur and Vouvray on the Loire, the most famous of which are those from Ackerman-Laurance. In recent years, dry white sparkling wines of good quality have been produced in Burgundy from white wines of Rully, where much of the red Sparkling Burgundy is made. Dry and sharp sparkling wines come from the Savoie, principally from the town of Seyssel; it is considered one of the best of the sparkling wines, after Champagne. From the Rhone comes the *vin mousseux* of Saint Péray, full and soft and rounded, generally ranking high with those who consider Champagne light and delicate. There are others, but these are the ones most worth noting, delicious if you like them—once having drunk Champagne.

Germany produces large quantities of sparkling wine called *Sekt*, popular in Europe when one can't afford Champagne, but wine that is rarely distinguished.

Every European country produces sparkling wines, but the only one apt to interest Americans is Asti Spumante from Italy's Piedmont. It is perhaps the best of the sweet sparkling wines, particularly pleasant with dessert, after an Italian dinner.

WINING BEFORE DINING

It wasn't so long ago that bands of merry peasants got together to tromp the grapes, pour the juice into big wooden tubs and then settle down to wait, hoping everything would turn out all right. Occasionally, somebody would get up and stir the bubbling juice with a paddle, then take a taste. I guess it tastes OK, he'd say, but maybe we should add something. Just leave it alone, a wise old man would say, it's going to be fine. Sometimes it was.

Usually there was something wrong. The wines were thin and sharp when there wasn't enough sun to plump the grapes, soft and flat when the grapes were too ripe. And the wine would keep changing, often turning to vinegar. To hide any bad tastes, herbs would be added, and spices. Many off-tastes could be masked by sweetness, first honey and then sugar. In the seventeenth century a man in Torino got the idea of adding something bitter along with the sweet and tossed in some artemisia blossoms. When he emigrated to Germany he took along his recipe. The Germans liked what he made and called it *vermut*, wormwood being their

word for the blossoms. Back in Italy, they took to
calling it Vermouth, the first aromatic wine to become
known internationally.

Again, it was the English who made Vermouth
fashionable, drinking it with gin, which they had taken

over from the Dutch. The scandal of London in Ho-
garth's day was the amount of gin drinking, and he
did a series of lithographs about its evils. When Vermouth came along, the fashionable drink was Gin-
and-It, half and half. The Italian Vermouth was only
about 20% alcohol so the drink was milder. The bitter-

sweet taste was supposed to make fewer drinks more satisfying, and maybe it did.

Gin-and-It was the first cocktail, opening the floodgates for the torrent that was devised after the turn of the century and during the time of the First World War, when a shortage of drinkables made it necessary to make a bottle of spirits go a long way. The pattern had been set by the Victorians, who took a fancy to exotically flavored wines and spirits, the forerunners of the aperitifs, cordials and liqueurs we have today. Many of the best were based on wine.

The first Vermouths were sweet, so it was no time at all until somebody decided to make a dry version. The "somebody" was the French around Marseille who couldn't bear to see all that business going to the Italians. French Vermouth became synonymous with

dry, Italian with sweet, and now every wine region makes them on a base of neutral wine. The main flavoring ingredients, in addition to wormwood, include anise and aloe, cardamon and camomile, bitter orange peel. These, and other peels, barks and berries, were used to make variations of Vermouth, each brand having its own distinctiveness. In Bordeaux, one firm increased the amount of orange peel, for example, to produce Lillet, now recognized as a fine aperitif wine.

Vermouth became so popular that the French, particularly, began experimenting to find something to impart a bitterness different than that of wormwood. They hit upon quinine, adding it to red wine, of which they had so much. The result was Dubonnet, which quickly became the most popular aperitif in France. Dubonnet was badly needed.

Europeans like to sit outdoors in warm weather. Paris café owners took to setting tables on the sidewalk, where people could order a drink and watch the passers-by. The custom goes back to the Greeks, but Parisians developed it into a way of life, with awnings and wicker chairs and quick service to attract strollers. As the Germans evolved the beer garden, the Viennese developed the coffee house, the English developed the pub, so the French glorified the sidewalk café.

But they needed a drink, something special to have in the afternoon, before going on to dinner—an aperitif, something appealing to whet the appetite. The answer was Dubonnet. Sweet but not too sweet, bitter but not too bitter, refreshing but not so satisfying that it would spoil the taste for dinner and for wine, Dubonnet had to be something that could be sipped or drunk quickly if you were hurried. These were the days before ice was easily available, so the drink had to quench thirst. Dubonnet suited the requirements so well that it has become the world's most popular aperitif, affected hardly at all by the scores of imitations and variations that have come along since.

The Spanish went about the matter of unstable wines in an entirely different way, their wines being more unstable than most of the others around the Mediterranean basin. They fermented their wines in

small casks and then sorted them, putting like ones together. Some developed a sort of yeast film on the surface of the wine that looked like little white flowers. They called it *flor* and blended these wines together. Others turned dark and had a strong fragrance; these were called *oloroso*. Some had a nutty smell and these were blended together and called *amontillado*, because they were like the wines from the region of Montilla. All the wines improved with age but varied widely from vintage to vintage, so they decided to blend one year with another, adding young wines to older ones. This called for a lot of barrels.

There wasn't enough room to leave the barrels lying around so they were stacked up. The youngest wines were put on top, the oldest on the bottom. When wine was needed it was drawn off from the oldest barrels, which were refilled from the younger. The tiers were called a *solera*, and sometimes they were stacked five barrels high. (The youngest wines went into separate tiers, called the cradle, the *criadera*, to blend together before being added to the top row of a *solera*.)

Some of the *soleras* are a century old, and older, so

The logic of how wines have come into being is fascinating. All the different kinds are confusing at first, but when you know how each is made, the result seems inevitable, the only thing that could be done to get the best out of the grapes. This is why a good wine, no matter how strange, seems to be so right, so much what it should be. This is why new wines are so exciting to taste; somebody may have figured out just the right thing to do with the grapes available. Wine making has quickly spread around the world during this century, from the slopes of Fujiyama to the Russian steppes, from the Blue Ridge of Virginia to the upper Rio Grande. People all over the world are becoming fascinated with wines, and new ones are coming on the market all the time, waiting to be discovered.

that there is a little of the oldest wine in every bottle. The old wines affect the aging process of the young wines, so that newer vintages take on the character of the older wines. By law, less than half of new wine can be added each year to a *solera*, so that the older character of the wine always predominates. Wines from one *solera* are blended with those from another, of course, always of the same type, each firm deciding just how the blending of their wines should go. A *fino* from one house will be quite different from the *fino* of another, and so it is for the other types.

No other system could guarantee consistency for the wines of Jerez, and the English were quick to discover them. They called them "Jerries," a cockney twist of the town name, which quickly came to be known as Sherry.

The wines were further stabilized for sea journeys by the addition of brandy, which brought up the alcoholic content to something like 20%. Such strong wines were traditionally sweet in earlier centuries, and so were the first Sherries. They were made so by boiling down grape juice to a syrup, then adding this to the finished wine. Fragrant *olorosos* lent themselves to this treatment, and so rich were the wines that the British called them Cream Sherries. The nutty taste of *amontillado* was allowed to predominate, only a little sweetening being added, less and less as time went by. The Spanish themselves preferred dry Sherries, the Finos, which tasted best when young and fresh and yeasty, cool from the cellar.

The Spanish love to nibble during the heat of the day, choosing to dine late at night, often at eleven o'clock. To fill the long void between meals, they have developed an astonishing variety of things to nibble on called *tapas*. Peanuts is one of them, tiny boiled shrimps in their shells another, olives a third—sometimes even

slices of sausage or ham, cheese, and whatever the proprietor can dream up for variation. Nothing tastes better with these *tapas* than a cool *fino*. All during the day,
the Spanish and those visiting them sit down in the
shade of a café, order a *fino* and little saucers of things
to eat. Any good roadside café is littered at the end
of the day with peanut shucks, shrimp shells and olive
pits, even though somebody is always sprinkling water
around and sweeping up.

Chilled dry Sherry, either *fino* or *amontillado*, is
the epicure's before-dinner drink, and while we have
adopted the Spanish *tapas* to serve with cocktails, we
have never taken to Spanish Sherries in place of mixed
drinks. If we drink Sherries at all, they are usually the
sweet styles, served with cakes or cookies.

The same unconcern is shown for *Porto*, once popular in the Colonies, designed to be drunk after dinner,
with walnuts or a bowl of fruit and perhaps some
cheese or crackers. The wine comes from the steep
valley of the Douro River in northern Portugal and
shipped from Oporto, where the wine is aged. The
process is similar to that of Jerez, young wines being
blended into *Ruby Porto*, older wines that have lost
some of their color becoming *Tawny Porto*.

They were called Port until a few years ago, when
the producers decided that there were so many poor
imitations that a distinctive name was needed so that the
real thing could be identified. They decided to adopt
the Portuguese word for the wine, and people are
getting used to calling for Porto when they want the
wine of the Douro. The wine is made by adding brandy
to stop fermentation, so that the natural sugar in the
grape is retained in the wine. Mostly made from red
grapes, there is also a White Porto from white grapes,
allowed to become dry as a way of producing a wine
suitable as an aperitif.

Most wines intended to be drunk before meals are on the sweet side, as are those based on wine. The exceptions are the dry Sherries and Champagne, which are preferred by epicures. That preference guides what wine lovers consider the best things to eat with before-dinner drinks—smoked meats like ham and dried sausages like salami, olives and other pickled or salted things, sliced raw vegetables like celery or radishes or carrots.

These are called *crudités* by the French, who are apt to serve them as a first course the way the Italians serve antipasto. Other things "out of the works," hors d'oeuvres, might be oysters or shrimp and mushrooms or pastry stuffed with spicy fillings. These last, though, like deviled eggs and the hot bits called canapés, are generally considered too filling to precede a meal and are the sort that taste best at cocktail parties that are not to be followed by dinner. Etiquette and fashionableness get involved with such edibles, and eating too many of them ruins the appetite for dinner and wine. Wine lovers like to keep it simple.

Breaking the cocktail habit isn't easy, with its dips and chafing dishes and little grilled goodies. Wine producers have been wracking their brains to come up with replacements for Scotch and soda, Bourbon and branch, Martinis, Bloody Marys, gin and tonic. They haven't been successful, except that people recently are showing more and more interest in Vermouths, aperitifs and Sherries, often served on-the-rocks or with soda.

Sweetness cuts thirst and stops hunger pangs, so makers of sweet wines have begun to talk about serving Sauternes and Rhine wines before meals. There is something of a trend toward serving dry white wines before meals, or even rosés, chilled as they come or made into punches. Red wines are reserved for dinner.

COMPARING WINES

Sense of smell is the best judge of wines, and by comparing two or three bottles at a time you can rapidly build up an inventory of bottlings you like. The trick is keeping track.

Ignorance is your best resource. Knowing nothing about a wine, you must decide for yourself whether you like it or not, and the easiest way is to compare it with a couple of others. The next time people are coming to dinner, open three different bottles ahead of time, pour an inch of each into glasses and decide which you prefer. Note the one you like best, then watch and see if your guests prefer the wine you do. When there is general agreement, you're on the track for finding good wines.

Wines change when exposed to the air, most wines being much better half an hour or so after the cork has been pulled. Once you've poured the wine, swirl it in the glass a few time before tasting it so that any superficial unpleasantnesses that can come from being enclosed—a possible gassiness or mustiness—can evaporate into the air. Then sniff each of the wines, deciding which one of the three you prefer.

The wines you've chosen can be far apart—perhaps

a white, a rosé and a red. They can be similar, even three wines from the same vineyard. With luck, all three may smell pleasant, a good sign to be confirmed by the looks and the taste.

A wine that's cloudy has something wrong with it, for a bottled wine is always clear, even brilliant. Wines clear themselves, sometimes in a few minutes, sometimes in a few months, but lack of clarity is a sign that the wine is in poor condition. You can expect all wines to be clear—so that you can see light from a window or a lamp or a candle through it.

The tastes are apt to be pleasant, too, a combination of bitterness and tartness, perhaps, balanced with fruitiness—a sign of a young wine. The wine may be bland and without freshness, not unpleasant but not interesting either, a sign of a wine that has been handled in a way to appeal to a wide audience. You may like them all.

Such a tasting may give a false impression of a wine, for it may be quite different with food. A wine that is almost too full of taste alone may be just right with a meal, and a bland wine may taste insipid and without interest. Tasting a wine both ways, and with others at the meal, will give you a much better idea of what you like.

To find out about wines most people think they have to go to formal tastings, try each one, take notes. Such tastings present so many wines to such crowds that it's hard to focus attention on a few of them, let alone all.

The simplest way is to try a trio, then drink them at a meal, with friends. Keep track of the wines that taste best, keeping the labels so you can identify the wines later. After a few months, you'll have a lengthy list.

SERVING A GREAT WINE

Trying a great one is the best way to find out what's so fascinating about wine. Some people get discouraged before they even find out about or taste something splendid. The wines everybody wants to discover are the table wines, those usually served with meals. Perhaps the best way to appreciate one is to serve it by itself, and not with dinner. In a sense, this is what a wine expert is apt to do. A great bottle deserves attention and may become lost in the excitement of a good dinner. The great wine is usually reserved for the cheese course, after the main part of the meal is done. Cheese is the perfect companion for wine. The only problem is that people may not have room for anything more, no matter how good the cheese and the wine. Appetite is essential for the enjoyment of wine, and thirst is needed too. To serve a great wine with the cheese, make the preceding dinner light, even skimpy.

Great wines call for simple foods; great dishes call for simple wines. It's no accident that the great chefs now cooking in Europe are all for serving young, fresh wines with their elaborate dishes.

The subtlety and range of taste in a great wine call

for dishes mild in taste, almost neutral, even bland. They can be rich with sauces but not sharp in taste. Pepper, spice, sour and salt all kill the taste of wine. Sweetness is particularly bad, making a wine taste sour. The best food to serve with a great wine is a plain steak or roast. The American preference for simple meat dishes may account for the growing enthusiasm for wines—because we can taste them so well.

A marvelous restaurant on the Coast often tries to encourage diners to try a great wine before the meal. Appetites are sharp then, according to the proprietor, and thus one is more apt to be thirsty and more likely to take interest in what's set before him. The wine can be served with a little pâté or with some slivers of ham or smoked turkey. Or with a few canapes or an hors d'oeuvre like a mushroom stuffed with minced chicken. Even thin slices of cheese on bits of bread. If it's a white wine, there are oysters and mussels and clams, served on the half shell or cooked and served cold. There is shrimp and crab meat and lobster and salmon. This way, the wine is set off at its best.

VINTAGES

There is always much discussion of vintages in the world of wines and much publishing of charts and ratings. Perhaps there shouldn't be. Regions and districts are far apart and what is good in one may be poor in another. Generalizations aren't much help.

The vintage year on the bottle is most useful to the buyer because he can find out how old the wine is. Many of the most popular wines, and almost all those that are relatively low in price, taste best when drunk young, within two or three years of their making, and the year on a bottle helps in avoiding those that are too old. Years are important on bottles of the great reds of Bordeaux and Burgundy, the Rhone and the Piedmont, because these wines should not be drunk before they are ready.

The fact of the matter is that the best vineyards do not bottle wines in poor years. Instead they sell their lots to the shippers for blending into regional wines. A thin sharp wine may become much more than palatable when it is softened with full wine from a better vintage. This makes non-vintage wines excellent bargains.

Wine makers have a special way of looking at vintages, considering them in terms of quantity. A vintner is never happy when he makes a small amount of wine of excellent quality because he won't have enough wine to satisfy his customers and the price will inevitably be high. He is happiest, perhaps, when he can make a lot of wine of good quality; it is too much to hope for a large yield *and* high quality.

This happens occasionally, however. Wines of superior quality were produced in 1970; in many districts it was also the largest vintage on record. Previously, the 1966 was a record harvest which had produced excellent wines; 1969 and 1971 were small harvests, although very good; 1968 was a disaster; 1967 was average. A brief list of vintages gives some idea.

PLENTIFUL	SMALL	AVERAGE
good to great	good to great	
1970	1971	1967
1966	1969	1964
1962	1961	

Even this list fails to give a proper picture: 1967 was a great year on the Rhone and on the Loire, 1964 was a great year in Germany.

Every vintage is touted as a great one, if there's any possibility of making people believe it. Most years, many regions make many good wines, but only tasting tells how good.

Some excellent wines can be found in years rated as "poor" or "average." Great vineyards get to be so considered because their wines are characteristic of the grapes from which they were made and the ground in which they grow, and because they can live a long time. They are characteristic of grape and soil even in poor years, although the wines may be too thin to last long. Chances are they will be ready quickly. Many wine lovers who don't want to spend vast amounts for good wines will buy the greatest vineyard wines from poor years and minor wines in great years. They may never have in their cellars wines that will last for twenty years, but they will have a steady supply of good wines drinkable three or four years after the vintage—and the occasional surprise bottle that will violate all the rules.

Unless you are planning to buy wines for keeping, there's not much point in paying attention to vintages.

WINE LANGUAGE

There are few words to apply to taste in any language, those that exist being general and vague because taste varies so subtly. The French have done the best job in trying to define taste specifically even though the words may sound strange and affected to American ears. There are a few such words that are helpful to know, but in most cases the ones you make up yourself are the most satisfactory.

Most people agree about the taste of wines. Putting

it into words, we generally fall back on similes that can be far-fetched but are mostly funny. And mostly negative. There's a strawlike taste in some white wines, for instance, that reminds me of a wet collie dog; a sort of chemical taste in watery wines that's like the smell of an old wad of chewing gum. One of the nicest I know is the description for the light wines of the Saar—glorious water—and once tasted, no description seems so apt. You can have a good time trying to describe wines, which are often likened to pretty girls, to music, to landscape. Here are a few words for wine with precise meanings—hard to describe but easy to recognize in the taste of wines.

ACIDITY   The fresh, sharp taste of a wine from the fruit acids that develop as a result of fermentation. A wine without sufficient acidity tastes flat and dull. Acidity declines as the wine ages.

AROMA   The fresh smell of a young wine, usually reminiscent of flowers or fruits. Simple and direct, it is often light but quite recognizable.

ASTRINGENT   The word is used to describe sharp tastes that do not come from acetic acid (see "sour").

BALANCE   A wine has balance if its qualities are poised, so that nothing seems to be too strong or too pronounced. All great wines are well-balanced; the taste seems to be a continuation of the bouquet.

BODY   A wine with body does not taste watery, but definitely of wine. A wine lacking in body will have a definitely thin taste, a characteristic that can be unpleasing.

BOUQUET   The various fruit acids and alcohols in a wine have different smells, mostly like flowers or fruits. These smells, together, are like a bouquet of flowers, most noticeable in red wines. Occasionally, a smell will dominate and a wine will be said to have a bouquet of raspberries or violets or mushrooms. Subtlety of bouquet develops as a wine ages, becoming a collection of aromas.

CLARET   A word long used for the red wines of Bordeaux.

DECANT   To pour wine, particularly to pour wine from a bottle where age has caused sediment to settle in the bottom. The trick is to pour off the wine in front of a light, stopping when the sediment threatens to trail out with the wine.

DRY   A word applied to wines without sweetness.

FRUITY   A wine that is rich in fruit acids and oils (mostly glycerine) from the grape has a juicy quality, the taste of fruit. It is particularly desirable in a young wine. Usually accompanied by goodly amounts of alcohol (sometimes as high as 14% in table wines), the fruitiness of a wine is augmented by the flowery and fruity tastes of the various alcohols in a wine. Fruitiness tends to decline as wine ages.

LITER   Metric measure about equal to a quart (1.06 American quarts). Wines in cask and vineyard yields are generally expressed in terms of hectolitres, which is 100 liters, about 25 gallons, or about 10 cases of wine of 12 bottles each.

MADERIZED   A wine that has taken on the character of the wines of Madeira is said to be maderized. It is the result of the action of air on the wine, particularly noticeable in white wines. The wines are said to have rusted, or oxidized, turning brown or orange. They taste of straw and have a brackish quality—unpleasant when light—replacing the fresh and fruity qualities the wine once possessed.

MATURE   Applied to a wine that has lost any bitterness (from tannin) or any sharpness (from fruit acids) and has picked up subtle and complex characteristics with the passage of time. (The alcohols in a wine are transformed into esters with time, which develop delicate flowery and fruity tastes.)

MUST   Term for unfermented grape juice.

NÉGOCIANT   French word for a wine shipper, as distinguished from a grower or vineyard owner.

NOSE   A casual taster's term meaning the bouquet, or collection of flowery and fruity smells, of a wine.

SEC   Not sweet. A wine is said to be dry when there is no sugary quality in the taste, although there may be some flowery or fruity characteristics.

SOUND   Another casual tasting term meaning that a wine has nothing wrong with it, such as an excess of acid or alcohol. Generally a sound wine is one that is healthy, without flaws and with the capability of developing with age.

SOUR   A sour wine is a bad wine, one that has turned to vinegar, a word that comes from *vin aigre*, sour wine. It is the result of bacteriological action in wine in contact with air, the result being acetic acid. Fruit acids in wine have sharp but not unpleasant tastes—citric acid like the taste of oranges or lemons, malic acid like the taste of apples—and these provide the wine with pleasant tastes. It is important to recognize the basic distinction.

TANNIN   Tannic acid, which has a bitter taste, develops in a wine from contact with the cask and from fermentation in the presence of stems, pips and skins. It is a natural element in all wines and, with the alcohol, keeps the wine from spoiling.

A SMALL WINE CELLAR

A nice sense of well-being comes from keeping a stock of wines on hand, even if the amount is only a case or so stuck in a closet. There's a feeling of luxury about having a choice among several bottles, and perhaps the best way to begin is to order a couple of mixed cases—a dozen different reds and a dozen different whites. Once embarked on buying by the case, it's easy to get carried away, particularly when you find several wines you like in the first batch. Here are some guide lines to keep you from pushing a good thing too far.

First of all, few of us have the proper space for storing wines over a period of years. For that, a cool and even temperature below 60° is desirable. Right away, we are generally limited to wines we will drink within the next couple of years. For all intents and purposes, these are wines for current drinking that may improve somewhat with a few quiet months in bottle. Fortunately for the purse, all such are relatively inexpensive, under four dollars a bottle.

Most wines taste better after a rest from the rigors

of bottling, shipping and handling. A week or so is enough for most but a month or so is better. Keeping a year's supply of wines on hand works out to be about right, guaranteeing a ready supply and an ample choice of good wines. The actual number depends on how often you serve wines. A European accustomed to drinking a bottle a day needs more storage space than a bachelor who might open a bottle a week.

Most families who become interested in wine are apt to serve it two or three times a week, opening an extra bottle or so when guests come for dinner. A case of twelve bottles might last a month, give or take a case or so over the course of a year. The most inexpensive way to buy them is to stock up each quarter, buying three or four cases during the seasonal sales. These take place right after New Year's when shops take inventory and offer odd bottles at bargain prices, before and after Lent, in late spring before vacations, and early in the fall.

Someone just starting a cellar would be wise to buy at least two mixed cases of reds and one of whites, averaging perhaps three dollars a bottle. The price range might be from twenty to forty dollars a case. When the next seasonal sale comes around, there should be several wines from the first batch that you might like to taste again. For the second purchase, you might buy split cases—six wines of one kind and six of another—perhaps eight or ten different wines altogether. When the third season rolls around, you will still have a stock of several cases of wine and be all set to make some new discoveries.

Eventually, three bottles out of four laid in your cellar will be red wines, if only because white wines are ready to drink when purchased, improving less in bottle than reds. The cost of such a cellar averages out to something less than four hundred dollars a year, perhaps a dollar a day. Even those who drink wines more frequently than two or three times a week, and entertain more often than once every few weeks, come to find that this sort of buying works well because they supplement their purchases by buying jug wines—those that are sold by the gallon or the half-gallon or in the double bottle, or magnum.

Here are three lists of twelve wines each, two of reds and one of whites. As mixed cases, they would provide a stock of 36 bottles. They could be bought in pairs, six wines to the case, for a total of 72 bottles. Buying split cases, six bottles of two wines to a case, would provide a stock of 216 bottles which would be a two-year supply for many people just becoming interested in wines. All of these are dry table wines, meant for meals. Sweet wines, fortified wines and the rest would be purchased in addition to the basic stock, and a mixed case of these is listed.

REGIONAL REDS

BORDEAUX.   Bordeaux Supérieur
Haut Médoc
Margaux
Saint Julien
Saint Estèphe
Graves
Saint Emilion
Pomerol

BURGUNDY	Pinot Noir Gamay
	Macon Rouge Supérieur
	Beaujolais Supérieur
	Beaujolais-Villages
RHONE	Côtes du Rhone Rouge
'	Châteauneuf-du-Pape
	Hermitage or Côte Rotie
LOIRE	Champigny, Chinon or Saint Nicholas
PORTUGAL	Dão
SPAIN	Rioja
ITALY	Barolo or Gattinara
	Barbaresco or Barbera
	Sassella, Grumello or Inferno
	Bardolino or Valpolicella
	Lambrusco
	Chianti

REGIONAL WHITES

PORTUGAL	Vinho Verde
BORDEAUX	Blanc Supérieur
BURGUNDY	Aligoté, Pinot Chardonnay Macon or Pouilly-Fuissé
LOIRE	Pouilly-Fumé, Vouvray or Muscadet
ALSACE	Sylvaner, Traminer, Gewürztraminer or Riesling
RHINELAND	Rheinpfalz or Rheinhessen
	Rheingau or Moselle
ITALY	Soave
	Orvieto
	Verdicchio
	Frascati
SPAIN	Rioja Bianco or Alella

PUNCHES, BOWLS & PITCHERS

Punches became popular in Europe during the last century as pleasant things to serve before ending an evening. The word comes from India, where it meant five, and the British adapted it to a formula for making a mixed drink—one part sour, one part sweet, one part strong, one part weak, with spices added to the base to bring everything together. Most punches are made to the same formula, whether they are served in a bowl or a pitcher.

Proportions vary. A white wine punch calls for a bottle of white wine, to which is added the juice of a lemon, a sprinkling of sugar, a jigger of brandy, a bottle of soda water, and ice instead of spice. All these can be juggled freely. A lemon can be peeled in a single long piece and this can be dropped into the wine to add zest. Some people like to add the peel and juice of an orange, which add some sweetness. A liqueur like Triple Sec can be added instead of the sugar and brandy, or Crème de Menthe might be used, either the white or the green kind. Instead of club soda, ginger ale or tea is sometimes used but these don't make as pleasing a drink. Peeled strips of cucumber can be added to each glass before pouring the punch; strawberries, raspberries or peaches can be floated in it, but these things clutter the drink and aren't as attractive as they seem to be. Simple punches are best.

WHITE WINE PUNCH

    1 bottle white wine, Sylvaner or Macon Blanc
    1 lemon, juice and peel
    1 tablespoon sugar, more or less to taste
    2 ounces brandy
    1 quart soda water
      ice

In a large pitcher or bowl, place a block of ice or a tray of ice frozen without the dividers. Pour in the bottle of wine, preferably chilled, add the lemon juice and peel, sprinkle over the sugar and stir. Pour in the brandy and the soda water. Ladle or pour into glasses garnished with a slice of lemon, a stick of cucumber or a plump strawberry or raspberry or slice of peach. The punch may be served on the rocks.

NOTE: *Bourbon, Scotch or any liqueur may be substituted for brandy, but the amount of sugar must be reduced accordingly, to taste.*

A red wine punch can be made in exactly the same way. If the juice of an orange and a lime is added, the result is the favorite Spanish summer drink, Sangria.

Champagne or sparkling wine can be used instead of the white wine. For a stronger punch, sparkling wine might be substituted for the soda water.

Hot punches are usually made with red wine. The

simplest of all is the French winter drink *vin chaud*. A portion of red wine is put to simmer in a saucepan and a sprinkle of sugar is added, perhaps with a clove (which may be stuck into a slice of lemon or orange) and a grating of nutmeg or cinnamon. When the wine is steaming it is poured in mugs, with a slice of lemon added. Often enough, the wine is simply heated by itself and poured into cups, the drinker adding the sugar to taste along with the slice of lemon. Nutmeg can be grated on top. In the more elegant cafes, a cinnamon stick is served with which to stir the *vin chaud*. It is not at all unusual to add a dash of brandy or Kirsch or whiskey to each cup.

HOT RED WINE PUNCH

    1 bottle red wine, Macon Rouge or Côtes du Rhone
    1 lemon sliced, each slice stuck with a clove
    1 tablespoon sugar
    ¼ teaspoon nutmeg, freshly grated if possible
       cinnamon sticks

Pour the wine into a saucepan and set over a low flame. Add lemon, sugar and nutmeg. Stir. When the wine has simmered gently for about a minute, and before it comes to a boil, remove from heat and pour into small mugs, seeing that a lemon slice goes into each cup. Serve with cinnamon sticks. (Cinnamon sticks may be rinsed and used over and over.)

    Cruz Garcia Real Saugria is a punch already mixed and bottled.

GLASSES

Just about any glass does fine for wine but the bigger it is, the better. The ideal shape has a tulip bowl on a stem, the bowl's size at least twice as large as the amount of wine you intend to put in it. The best glasses are considered to be those that are half chimney, so that the aroma from the wine is contained and the drinker can get a good whiff of it. The mouth of the glass is generally smaller than the bowl, rounding in so that the wine can be swirled to release more of the aroma, and not spill. The glass should be large enough to hold eight ounces or more when filled, although three ounces is generally considered to be the average serving.

Such glasses are what's needed for the best wines, the stem making it easy to hold so that fingers don't obscure the wine when you want to look at it. Wines are something to see, for the colors are so infinitely varying. Even the most ordinary wine has a striking color and a large stemmed glass makes it more appealing.

Any glass will do, of course, and any shape, but

the glass itself should be clear so that the wine can be seen. There was once a fashion for colored glass and for fancifully etched ones, but modern glasses are austerely plain so that all the decoration comes from the wine and its reflection on the table. Even short and squatty tumblers show off the wine better than decorated glasses do.

Two wines are better than one at a dinner, if only because it is nice to taste wines against each other and with different foods. To keep wines from getting mixed up when two are served at the same time, it is helpful to have two sizes of glasses. People can usually manage to keep two wines separate, even when they are both red, however. Keeping them straight becomes a problem only when several wines are served—and there's a nice feeling of anticipation when one sees a table set with two glasses at each place, ready for a succession of wines.

Cleaning wine glasses spotlessly is a cinch. They should be washed first before anything else. Dunk them in good hot water to which a dishwashing detergent (not soap, which can leave a film) has been added and wash off any marks with an absolutely clean dishwashing brush. Immediately rinse each glass in turn under piping hot water and let it drain upside down until it's dry.

To cut down on breakage of fragile stemware: Don't jounce good wine glasses around in a dishwasher, do them by hand—slowly; To avoid chipping, rinse them under a faucet to which a rubber spray has been attached. Place upside down to drain on a clean dish towel on a flat surface well out of the way of the kitchen hustle-bustle; set their edges just barely out over the edge of the spread-out dish towel so that air can circulate inside each glass.

Glasses should be stored on shelves mouths up.

APPENDIX

This is a book to read, but you can also use it as a helpful guide to all those wine bottles on the shelves of your neighborhood shop.

Feel free to carry it into the store to assist you in your hunt for good values in imported wines. The list that follows is included for that purpose. You'll be surprised at how soon all the names become familiar.

RED BURGUNDY WINES

*Enjoy them with steaks, chops, roasts
and other hearty entrees.*

BEAUJOLAIS-VILLAGES, JOSEPH DROUHIN
(Bo-jho-lay Vee-lahj Droo-ahn) Elegant, light and quite fruity.

DOMAINE DE LA ROMANEE, BICHOT
(Doe-man Day Li Romah-ay) One of the rarest of the red Burgundies—rich, full character, lingering huge bouquet.

SANTENAY, BICHOT
(Sahn-ten-aye) Superbly conditioned, sound and well-balanced.

FLEURIE, BICHOT
(Flew-ree) Robust, full, with a bouquet to match its body.

POMMARD, BICHOT
(Poe-mar) Soft, full-bodied and round describes one of the finest wines of the world.

PINOT NOIR, BICHOT
(Pee-no Nwar) One of the finest of red wine grapes, produces all the great red Burgundies.

COTE DE BEAUNE-VILLAGES, DROUHIN
(Coat d'Bone Vee-lajh) A soft, full-bodied red wine of brilliant ruby colour and lovely bouquet.

VOLNAY, JOSEPH DROUHIN
(Voll-nay Droo-ahn) A light distinguished and extremely pleasant dinner wine with an unusual fruity vitality.

VOLNAY-CLOS DES CHENES, JOSEPH DROUHIN
(Voll-nay Klo d'Shane) Soft, fine and velvety with a lovely colour and bouquet . . . at its best with full flavoured meat.

POMMARD, JOSEPH DROUHIN
(Poe-mahr Droo-ahn) A beautifully balanced, rich, ruby Burgundy . . . firm, vigorous and long lived.

CLOS DE VOUGEOT, JOSEPH DROUHIN
(Klo d'Voo-joe Droo-ahn) An elegant red wine . . . rich, full flavoured with a distinguished ancestry.

CLOS DE VOUGEOT, FAIVELEY
(Klo duh Voo-joe Fay-ve-lee) An elegant red wine . . . rich, full flavoured with a generous bouquet.

MERCUREY "CLOS DES MYGLANDS"
(Mair-cue-RAY Klo Day Mee-Glahn) Distinctive, generous red wine made entirely from the small Pinot Noir grapes of Burgundy.

NUITS SAINT GEORGES, "CLOS DE LA MARECHALE" FAIVELEY
(N'wee San Jhorjh Fay-ve-lee) A "Premier Grand Cru" of the Cote de Nuits . . . beautiful, rich, full-flavoured.

GEVREY-CHAMBERTIN, FAIVELEY
(Jev-ray Sham-bair-tan Fay-ve-lee) Rich, full-flavoured, big in every way . . . fragrance, body and palate.

MACON, BICHOT
(Mah-cawn) Lively flavour and bouquet.

BEAUJOLAIS, BICHOT
(Bo-sho-lay) Fresh, fruity and most popular Burgundy.

BEAUJOLAIS VILLAGES, BICHOT
(Bo-sho-lay Vee-la-jez) Fine character with a fruity flavour.

CHATEAU DE BUFFAVENT-BEAUJOLAIS SUPERIEUR, BICHOT
(Shot-toe d'Buff-aw-vawn) Marvelously well rounded wine worthy of the ancient name Buffavent.

CHATEAU DE MERCEY BOURGOGNE ROUGE, BICHOT
(Shot-toe d'Mair-say) Soft and fruity tasting.

MOULIN-A-VENT, BICHOT
(Moo-lon ah Vawn) King of Beaujolais wines. Receives much character from its bigness.

COTE DE BEAUNE VILLAGES, BICHOT
(Coat d'Bone Ve-la-jez) A marvelous blending of wines from the Cote de Beaune. Soft and fruity in taste.

COTE DE NUITS VILLAGES, BICHOT
(Coat d'Nwee Vee-la-jez) A blending of fine wines from the Cote de Nuits. Full and well rounded.

GEVREY CHAMBERTIN, BICHOT
(Jev-ray Shawm-bear-tawn) Generous and full-flavoured with a fine finish.

VOSNE ROMANEE, BICHOT
(Vone-Ro-ma-nay) Deep colour with a rich taste.

NUITS SAINT GEORGES, BICHOT
(Nwee San Shorsh) Generous in flavour and bouquet.

VOSNE-ROMANEE, DOMAINE DU CLOS FRANTIN, E.B.
(Vone Ro-ma-nay) A magnificent wine with a robe of rubies and a finesse to please any palate.

**VOSNE-ROMANEE LES MALCONSORTS, DOMAINE DU
CLOS FRANTIN, E.B.**
(Vone Ro-ma-nay Lay Mal-cawn-sor) One of the most sumptuous wines of Burgundy with a silky body and a huge bouquet.

ECHEZEAUX DOMAINE DU CLOS FRANTIN, E.B.
(Esh-shay-zol) Its lightness of body surprises because of its subtlety of power.

GRANDS ECHEZEAUX, DOMAINE DU CLOS FRANTIN, E.B.
(Grawn Esh-shay-zo) Its lingering aftertaste makes it even more desirable than its little sister, the Echezeaux.

CLOS DE VOUGEOT, DOMAINE DU CLOS FRANTIN, E.B.
(Cloh duh Voo-sho) A splendid wine with an incomparable velvety and rich bouquet.

CHAMBERTIN, DOMAINE DU CLOS FRANTIN, E.B.
(Shawm-bear-tawn) A big wine full of vitality and bouquet.

RICHEBOURG, DOMAINE DU CLOS FRANTIN, E.B.
(Reesh-borg) Ranks among the finest wines of France along with La Romanee.

RED BORDEAUX WINES

CHATEAU TRIMOULET, ST. EMILION GRAND CRU CLASSE
(Sha-toe Tree-moo-lay) Generous, full-bodied and of a darkly brilliant colour . . . well balanced with an excellent bouquet and palate.

MEDOC, DREYFUS-ASHBY SELECTION
(May-dock) Light in body, brilliant in colour and unique for its delicate fragrance and delightful palate.

CHATEAU BEAULIEU BORDEAUX SUPERIEUR
(Sha-toe Bo-l'yeu) Robust, fruity and clean, this excellent Bordeaux Superieur is a real delight.

SAINT-JULIEN, DREYFUS-ASHBY SELECTION
(San Jhoo-l'yan) Rich in colour and bouquet, yet retains the finesse and soft palate that makes fine claret a world favourite.

CHATEAU SAVOIE BORDEAUX
(Shah-toe Sah VWA) The lovely colour and soft fruitiness makes it most enjoyable.

CHATEAU VIEUX-ROBIN MEDOC
(Sha-toe Vee-uh ROH-ban) An exceptionally elegant, light red wine of charming flavour and delicate fragrance.

CHATEAU RESPIDE, GRAVES ROUGE
(Sha-toe RAY-speed) This is an excellent tastemate for medium flavoured entrees and cheeses. Has a rich colour and rather soft palate.

CHATEAU KIRWAN MARGAUX GRAND CRU
(Sha-toe Kir-WAHN) This extraordinary red wine has the delicacy and softness of the great wines of Margaux.

BORDEAUX SUPERIEUR, BICHOT
(Bor-doe) A full flavoured wine with pleasing aftertaste.

MEDOC, BICHOT
(May-dock) Dry, medium body, well balanced.

CABERNET SAUVIGNON, BICHOT
(Cah-bear-nay Sov-veen-yawn) The noble grape variety used for the great red wines of Bordeaux.

ST. EMILION, BICHOT
(Sawn Ay-mee-lee-yon) Full bodied and most robust of the Bordeaux wines.

MARGAUX, BICHOT
(Mar-go) Marvelous bouquet and pleasantly dry.

ST. JULIEN, BICHOT
(Sawn Ju-lee-en) Charming and distinguished in flavour and bouquet.

CHATEAU MOULIN DE MARC GRAVES ROUGES, BICHOT
(Moo-lon day Mar) Remarkable flavour with a fine bouquet.

CHATEAU LAFFITTE CANTEGRIC, LISTRAC BICHOT
(Lah-feet Cawn-tah-gree) A fine Medoc combining delicacy and finesse
with a fine bouquet.

CHATEAU CORBIN VIEILLE TOUR, SAINT EMILION, BICHOT
(Cor-bin Vee-ay Tour) Generous and full bodied personality combined
with great finesse.

CHATEAU DES TUILERIES, BICHOT
(Shot-toe Day Twee-lay-ree) Splendid red wine in the classic Bordeaux
tradition. Full, rich distinguished.

ROSÉ WINES

*Fresh and fragrant, delicious
with any type of food.*

ROSE d'ANJOU, DREYFUS-ASHBY SELECTION
(Ro-zay Dawn-zhoo) This light-bodied and fragrant wine goes delightfully
with all kinds of food.

TAVEL DELAS FRERES
(Tah-vel Day-la Frair) A delightful all purpose pink wine generally considered the best of the French rosés.

MATEUS ROSE
(Ma-toos) Outstanding pink-amber Portuguese wine of unusual taste . . .
America's most popular imported wine.

ROSE d'ANJOU, ACKERMAN-LAURANCE
(Ro-zay Dawn-zhoo) Fragrant, soft and smooth. Excellent any time.

CABERNET d'ANJOU, ACKERMAN-LAURANCE
(Cah-bear-nay Dawn-zhoo) Delightfully fresh and dry.

MACON ROSE, BICHOT
(Mah-cawn Ro-zay) A certain delicate lightness which will suit all food.

TAVEL ROSE, BICHOT
(Tah-vell Ro-zay) A pleasant fragrance and distinctive flavour.

RED RHONE WINES

CHATEAUNEUF DU-PAPE DELAS FRERES
(Shah-toe-noof Doo-pop Day-la Frair) Robust, full flavored Rhone red
wine with rich bouquet for use with hearty food.

COTES DU RHONE, BICHOT
(Coat du Rhone) Soft, rich and round.

CHATEAUNEUF DU PAPE, BICHOT
(Shah-toe-noof Doo-pop) A robust wine that is supple and flavourful.

LOIRE RED WINES

CHINON, ACKERMAN-LAURANCE
(She-nawn) Magnificent soft and velvety red wine from the Loire region.

WHITE TABLE WINES

*Served chilled to add pleasure to
fish, fowl, veal and other light dishes.*

CHABLIS PREMIER CRU, JOSEPH DROUHIN
(Shah-blee Prem-yair Kru, Droo-ahn) An excellent example of this wine
at its remarkable best . . . clean and crisp.

POUILLY-FUISSE, JOSEPH DROUHIN
(Pwee-yee Fwee-say Droo-ahn) A dry, rather vigorous white wine with
good colour and bouquet.

MEURSAULT, JOSEPH DROUHIN
(Mair-so, Droo-ahn) A full flavoured dry white wine with a lovely golden
colour and excellent bouquet.

SOLEIL BLANC, JOSEPH DROUHIN
(So-lay Blahn, Droo-ahn) Pleasant, quite dry white Burgundy with a
charming bouquet and light straw colour.

MEURSAULT-PERRIERES, JOSEPH DROUHIN
(Mair-so-Pear-ry Aire, Droo-ahn) Fine, full-bodied white table wine rated
as one of the best in all France.

CLOS DE MOUCHES BLANC, JOSEPH DROUHIN
(Klo d'Moosh-Blahn, Droo-ahn) Made exclusively of white pinot grapes,
exceptionally flavoursome, soft, rich, dry.

PULIGNY-MONTRACHET, JOSEPH DROUHIN
(Poo-lee nyee Maw-ra-shay Droo-ahn) One of the finest dry white wines
of all France . . . great quality and richness.

PINOT CHARDONNAY, BICHOT
(Pee-no-Shar-doe-nay) Noble grape variety of the great white burgundies.

CHATEAU DE MERCEY BOURGOGNE ALIGOTE, BICHOT
(Sha-toe duh Mair-say) Dry with a light pleasant taste. At its best when
very young.

PETIT CHABLIS, BICHOT
(Puh tee Shab-lee) Light in body with a delicate taste.

CHABLIS, BICHOT
(Shab-lee) Medium body with exceptional dryness.

CHABLIS PREMIER CRU, BICHOT
(Shab-lee Prem-me-ya crew) Marvelous bouquet with a full flinty flavour.

POUILLY-FUISSE, BICHOT
(Pwee-yee Fwee-say) Delicate with a balance in dryness.

PULIGNY MONTRACHET, BICHOT
(Poo-lee Nyee Maw-ra-shay) Excellent dry, soft flavour. Boasts a huge personality.

MEURSAULT, BICHOT
(Mere-so) Soft and luxurious taste.

CORTON-CHARLEMAGNE, BICHOT
(Cor-tawn Sharl-mawn) One of the two greatest white burgundies and quite rare. Rich in flavour and bouquet with great breeding.

CHABLIS PREMIER CRU-LES BEUGNONS, BICHOT
(Prem-me-yea crew Lay Boy-yon) An excellent white Burgundy, dry, soft and rich in flavour.

CHABLIS PREMIER CRU LES LYS, BICHOT
(Prem-me-yea crew Lay Lees) Delicate with a beautiful balance in dry-ness, taste, bouquet.

CHABLIS GRAND CRU-LES PREUSES, BICHOT
(Grawn crew Lay Pruh-z) Very flavorsome . . . wonderfully soft and dry.

CHABLIS GRAND CRU-LES VAUDESIRS, BICHOT
(Grawn crew Lay Vo-day zeer) Exceptionally clean, crisp with just the right dryness.

CHABLIS GRAND CRU-LES CLOS, BICHOT
(Grawn crew Lay clo) A lovely, delicate wine, dry with delightful bouquet.

CHABLIS GRAND CRU-MOUTONNE, BICHOT
(Grawn crew Moo-tawn) Full-bodied, rich but dry . . . outstanding in flavour.

LAFORET MACON-VILLAGES, JOSEPH DROUHIN
(La-for-ay May-cong Vee-lahj, Droo-ahn) An elegant, gracious wine so well appreciated for its true Chardonnay fragrance and flavor. Well-liked with sole, trout, or any fine fish.

WHITE BORDEAUX WINES

CHATEAU BELLEVUE, SAUTERNES
(Sha-toe Bel-view) Beautiful, golden-brown colour, luscious sweet flavour, perfect with or instead of dessert.

CHATEAU JACQUET, BORDEAUX
(Sha-toe Jha-kay) Elegant white wine . . . clean, soft and semi-dry.

CHATEAU MALLEPRAT, GRAVES
(Sha-toe Mahl-eh-prah Grahv) Crisp and dry with a fine balance of palate and aroma.

SAUTERNES, DREYFUS-ASHBY SELECTION
(So-tairn) A rich, sweet wine with a fully developed character and an exceptional bouquet.

GRAVES, DREYFUS-ASHBY SELECTION
(Grahv) A thoroughly enjoyable dry white wine . . . perfectly balanced, with fine colour, bouquet and palate.

GRAVES SUPERIEURES SEC, BICHOT
(Grahv) Clean and fresh with a fruity bouquet.

SAUVIGNON BLANC, BICHOT
(Soh-veen-yawn Blawn) An exceptional grape variety used for the finest white wines of Bordeaux.

CHATEAU MOULIN DE MARC, GRAVES SUPERIEURES SEC, BICHOT
(Moo-lon day Mar) Magnificent, dry wine bottled at the Chateau In Graves.

BARSAC, BICHOT
(Bar-sack) Gracious and delightfully sweet.

SAUTERNES, BICHOT
(So-tairn) Soft and sweet tasting with a lovely bouquet.

HAUT SAUTERNES, BICHOT
(Oh So-tairn) Luscious, sweet and full bodied with a fine aftertaste.

WHITE ALSATIAN WINES

SYLVANER, HUGEL
(Sil-vah-ner Hyou-gel) Superb clean, dry, fruity wine may be served with any light meal or as an aperitif.

RIESLING RESERVE EXCEPTIONNELLE, HUGEL
(Rees-ling Ray-Sairv Ess-sept-shun-Ell, Hyou-gel) A distinguished and fragrant dry wine of great breeding, with a clean and delicate flavour.

TRAMINER, HUGEL
(Trah-mee-ner Hyou-gel) Deep, rich, lingering flavour and pronounced bouquet. Big enough to serve with hearty dishes. Medium dry.

GEWURTZTRAMINER, HUGEL
(Geh-vurtz-trah-mee-ner Hyou-gel) This flowery, spicy dry white wine shows a remarkable balance of bouquet, colour and palate.

WHITE LOIRE WINES

LADOUCETTE-POUILLY FUME
(La-doo-set Pwee-yee Fu-may) An extremely dry wine of great finesse and warm gaiety, with springtimelike freshness and perfect balance.

MUSCADET DE L'HYVERNIERE
(Moo-skah-day duh Lee-vairn-yair) A light delicate wine young and fresh. Excellent with oysters and all other seafood.

CHENIN d'ANJOU, ACKERMAN-LAURANCE
(Shay-nan Dawn-zhoo) A fine fresh varietal wine from the Loire Valley noble wine grapes.

MUSCADET, ACKERMAN-LAURANCE
(Muhs-cad-day) Fresh, delicate and dry with lovely bouquet.

SANCERRE, ACKERMAN-LAURANCE
(San-sair) Fresh, fruity and lively.

SAUVIGNON, ACKERMAN-LAURANCE
(Soh-veen-yawn) Light bodied with zestful full flavour.

VOUVRAY, ACKERMAN-LAURANCE
(Voo-vray) Smooth and soft, medium dry. Famous for its extreme delicacy.

WHITE SPARKLING LOIRE WINES

BLANC DE BLANCS, ACKERMAN-LAURANCE
(Blawn duh Blawn) Fresh bouquet, fruity and clean flavour.

BLANC "1811," ACKERMAN-LAURANCE
(Blawn) Fresh and zesty with a heady bouquet.

ROSE "1811" ACKERMAN-LAURANCE
(Ro-zay) Delicate, light bodied, pleasingly fresh.

PORTUGUESE WINES

MATEUS ROSE
(Ma-toos) Outstanding pink-amber Portuguese wine of unusual character . . . America's most popular imported wine.

GRAO VASCO, RED
(Gay-oh Vas-ko) An invigorating red wine full in body, deep ruby in colour, fruity in flavour.

CASAL GARCIA, VINHO VERDE
(Cas-sal Gar-see-ah Veen-yo Vair-day) Smooth, medium dry white wine, one of the most popular in Portugal . . . light, refreshing and thirst-quenching.

MATEUS SPIRAL
Fresh, lightly sparkling, pink-amber wine in a distinctive crock of spiral design. Joyous, festive.

GRAO VASCO, WHITE
(Gray-oh Vas-ko) Popular Portuguese wine, deliciously dry, perfect accompaniment to fish and fowl.

ITALIAN WINES

RIVERA BIANCO, VINTAGE (WHITE)
(Ri-vera Bee-awn-co) Light bodied, crisp and fresh tasting.

RIVERA ROSE, VINTAGE
(Ri-vera Ro-zay) The ideal wine any time, light in body, medium dry.

RIVERA ROSSO, VINTAGE (RED)
(Ri-vera Ro-so) Vigorous, full bodied, with a rich bouquet.

VERDICCIO CLASSICO DEL CASTELLI DI JESI
(Vair-deek-ee-o) Straw-coloured light wine, dry, with a delightful after-taste, wonderful with appetizers, fish.

ROSSO PICENO
(Ross-o Pee-cheen-o) Ruby-red, pleasantly dry, full winey aroma. A famous old wine of the hills.

BARDOLINO, NEGRAR
(Bar-doe-leen-o) An outstanding red wine produced in the Verona region, dry, distinctive, delicious.

VALPOLICELLA, NEGRAR
(Val-pole-ee-chella) One of the best Italian reds, an excellent choice with roasts and broiled meats.

SOAVE, NEGRAR
(Swah-vay) Classical dry white wine . . . superb with hors d'oeuvres, fish or egg dishes.

RISERVA CASTELLO DI VERRAZZANO CHIANTI CLASSICO
(Kee-yonti) Dry, harmonic and velvety taste, suitable for dishes of game and strong cheese.

CHIANTI CLASSICO VERRAZZANO
(Kee-yonti) Ruby-coloured wine, with garnet shades, deliciously dry. Fine with roasts or red and white meats.

VINO BIANCO SECCO TOSCANO VERRAZZANO
(Vee-no Bee-anco) Brilliant straw-coloured wine. Its taste is dry and generous. Excellent with fish, sea-food.

VERRAZZANO ROSE
Rose-coloured and brilliant wine, delicate with dry taste.

CORTESE FRANCO-FIORINA
(Kor-tay-zee) Straw yellow in color. Large bouquet, dry and full body. Especially recommended for fish.

BAROLO FONTANAFREDDA
(Buh-role-oh) A red wine of great body and bouquet. Aged up to 15 years, this is recommended for meats, game and cheese.

BARBERA FRANCO-FIORINA
(Bar-bair-uh) Deep ruby red wine, dry yet well rounded. Suitable for roasted meats and meat dishes in general.

BARBARESCO FONTANAFREDDA
(Bar-ba-ress-ko) Ruby red color, and well developed aroma. Fine with roasts, game and cheese.

GRIGNOLINO FRANCO-FIORINA
(Green-yo-leen-o) Light ruby red color. Specially suitable for Italian hors d'oeuvres, fried meats or boiled meats.

NEBBIOLO FRANCO-FIORINA
(Neb-ee-o-lo) Ruby red color with a very delicate aroma. Body is firm and full of character; for red meats and game birds.

ASTI SPUMANTE FONTANAFREDDA
(As-tee Spoo-mahn-tee) World famous sparkling wine from Italy. Elegant, star-bright, with a touch of natural sweetness. Splendid with all foods and desserts.

FRATELLI LAMBRUSCO
(Frah-telly Lom-broos-ko) A friendly, light, "tingly" red wine, hearty and full of taste.

GERMAN WINES

LIEBFRAUMILCH MADONNA
(Leeb-frow-milsh) Perhaps the very finest of all Liebfraumilch wines. Elegant, mild, superb true character.

ZELLER SCHWARZE KATZ, VALKENBERG
(Tseller Shvartzeh kots) The official, cork-branded white wine of the region. 100% riesling for fullest flavour.

MOSELBLUMCHEN, VALKENBERG
(Mo-zel-blum-shen) Delightfully fresh and "tingly" white wine of outstanding quality.

RUDESHEIMER ROSENGARTEN, VALKENBERG
(Roy-dis-hy-mer) One of the best-liked light wines of the Rhine. Favored for its charming flavour.

NIERSTEINER DOMTHAL, GUNTRUM
(Neer-shtine-er) White, light-bodied Rhine wine at its flavourful best.

PIESPORTER MICHELSBERG, GUNTRUM
A very popular Moselle, pale, dry, with a fine clear taste.

JOHANNISBERGER RIESLING, GUNTRUM
Fresh, flowery bouquet in a soft, light white wine.

LAUBENHEIMER, GUNTRUM
Appealing aroma, quite dry, always dependable for fine taste.

ZELLER SCHWARZE KATZ, GUNTRUM
(Tseller shvartzeh kots) Excellent Moselle, light, crisp, flavourful.

BERNKASTELER RIESLING, GUNTRUM
An always popular choice with a lovely flavour and aroma. Light, refreshing.

JUMPING DEER LIEBFRAUMILCH, VINTAGE
(Leeb-frau-milsh) Agreeable, pleasant tasting, medium dry wine of the Rhine.

JUMPING DEER ZELLER SCHWARZE KATZ, VINTAGE
(Tseller-shvartzeh-kots) Refreshing, delicate taste and bouquet from a top Riesling region.

JUMPING DEER MOSELBLUEMCHEN, VINTAGE
(Mo-zell-bloom-shen) Charming white, dry wine with a pleasing "spritz" quality.

JUMPING DEER NIERSTEINER DOMTAL, VINTAGE
Full-bodied Rhine wine with a distinctive, fruity flavour.

SPANISH WINES

CRUZ GARCIA REAL SANGRIA
Today's most popular Spanish import . . . made with fine Rioja wine and fresh citrus juice. Delicious.

SIGLO VINTAGE—RED BURGUNDY
Imported in a burlap-wrapped bottle. Rich Rioja wine with fine distinctive flavour.

SIGLO VINTAGE—WHITE CHABLIS
Remarkably fine Spanish wine in the famous burlap-wrap bottle.

SIGLO VINTAGE—GARNACHO ROSE
Spain's finest pink wine, light and delicious. In the well-known burlap wrap bottle.

AGE—RED BURGUNDY
(Ah-hay) Traditional Spanish vintage wine in smart, tri-corner bottles. Very pleasant and flavorful.

AGE—WHITE CHABLIS
(Ah-hay) Traditional Spanish white vintage wine with full, zesty flavor.

AGE—ROSE
(Ah-hay) Lively, light, pink vintage wine in the traditional Spanish character.

SPARKLING WINES

KRUG CHAMPAGNE
(Kroog) Recognized by connoisseurs the world over as the finest champagne available. The delightful choice before, during or after meal. Always in limited supply. Rich, dry, distinguished.

HEIDSIECK MONOPOLE CHAMPAGNE
(Hide-sik) Very elegant, very gracious . . . and very lovely to the taste.

SPARKLING BURGUNDY, BICHOT
A full-bodied sparkling red wine preferred by many people with heartier tastes.

ACKERMAN BLANC DE BLANC
Charming Loire sparkling white wine—fresh, fruity, zesty flavour.

ACKERMAN SPARKLING ROSE
A sparkling pink wine that goes with everything, any time. Medium dry, altogether delightful.

ASTI SPUMANTE, FRANCO-FIORINA
World famous sparkling wine from Italy. Elegant, star-bright, with a touch of natural sweetness. Splendid with all foods and desserts.

KRUG CHAMPAGNE, VINTAGE
The wine of a single and exceptional year which combines the rich, distinguished style of Krug with the delicate individuality of a great vintage.

KRUG CHAMPAGNE "BLANC DE BLANCS," VINTAGE
The elegant characteristics of the noble Chardonnay grape, the qualities of an exceptional year and the rich, distinguished style of the House of Krug all act in concert to make this unique wine truly majestic.

APERITIFS (APPETIZER WINES)

Prelude to a memorable meal.

LILLET (WHITE OR RED)
(Lee-lay) One of the truly fine aperitif wines of France . . . tantalizing, unique, subtle flavour and aroma. Most enjoyable on the rocks.

DUBONNET (RED OR BLONDE)
(Doo-bow-nay) The best known aperitif in the world . . . deservedly. Enjoy "the flavour of Paris" in every drop.

STOCK VERMOUTH (SWEET OR DRY)
Italy's great gift to gourmets everywhere . . . her finest wines infused with marvelous herbs and spices for taste perfection.

INDEX

WINE NOTES

WINE NOTES

WINE NOTES